MIDLIFE
calm

An Alternative to
Midlife Crisis

Krista M. Powers

VITALITY
buzz, bliss + books

Contents

Intention and Dedication

This book is dedicated to the part of each of us bubbling up from within. It was written with the intention of creating curiosity in individuals, sparking conversations, cultivating new paradigms, shifting cultural norms, and healing our world. All of which happens one human at a time.

And to my Godchildren – Nathan, Theo, Paul, and Skylar – this book is also dedicated to you. Create an entire life of calm, you precious beings!

"You are important and powerful." I often share this sentiment with the people in my life. Individually and as a community, we radiate when we embrace this simple and beautiful truth. As the people who preordered and breathed life into this book, please also receive this message. To every VATRON, *you* are important and powerful. Namaste.

Ehab Abdalla, Ahmat Acyl, Nic Alessandrini, Warner and Jen Allen, Lauren Almquist, Ken Ashby & Maris Segal, Jackson Athey, Jean and Mike Badik, James Barker, Nathan Barker, Taylor Barker, Deana Barone, Peter and Michelle Barrett, Alicia Bauer, Amy Benetti, Lori Beran, Jeanne Bilyeu, Jenni Blake, Fr. John Blaser, Ashley Blevins, Lisa Boh, Diana and Steve Bosse, Shannon Braun, Logan Brown, Meghan Brown, Raegan Brown, Marge Brown, Patricia Brundage, Suzanne Bryan, Barbie Burnett, Amy Carpenter, Ilona Castro, Carri Chandler, Karl Coiscou, Kristin Cooley, Holly Cousino, Jerry Craft, Sarah Creighton, Dave Culver, Jess Cybrowski, Richard Danford, Jennifer Danner, Tracy Davis, Ron and Dianne Davis, Kim Denzler, Rachel DesRochers, Sue and Mark Dickey, Frank DiLallo, Diane Dixon, Catie Doebler, Erik Dominguez, Jesse Dunbar, Reba Dysart, Allison Edwards, Deanna Edwards, Bridget Eichhold, Emily Elma, Marissa Esterline, Adam and Chloe Fairchild, Jean Ann Fairchild, Keith Fairchild, Tyler and Erica Fairchild, Kathy Farfsing, Bobbie Farley, Amy and John Fecker, Nikole Fernandez Rivera, Maggie Ferrara, Nan Fischer, Mark Fisher, Coen Flerlage, Lane Flerlage, Patrick Flerlage, Allison Fournier, Carolyn Frank, Jennifer Frank, Valorie Frantz, Sarah Frey, Julie Friebel, Jennifer Gainer, Dante Gapultos, Christian and Cody Gausvik, Cindy Geer, Myrna Gonzalez, Bill Good, Laura Gramenelles, Rachelle Gray, Layne and Jeff Haas, Janet Hahn, Heather Hallman, Josie Haney, Lauren and Mark Hannah, Christopher Hernandez, Lisa and Abel Hernandez, Richard Hernandez, Herman and Dorothy Heuring, Rhiannon Hoeweler, Holly Hoff, Angie Homoelle, Julie Hopkins, Forrest Horn, Bill and Sandy Hostler, Dana Hubka, Zac and Elizabeth Huffman, Jay Humphrey, Amy Hunter, Connie Isbell, Megan Mitchell & Izzy Wilson, Lynda Jackson, Rachel Jackson-Gordon, Cheryl Jeffers, Adam Johnston, Carolyn Karageorges, John Kays, Amy Keiderling, Heather Kendall, David Kendrick, Sue and Tom Knippen, Danika Koopmans, Holly Krills, MaryBeth Lacy, Angele Lamothe, Jodi Landers,

one

I quit my job.

I was a single, 42-year-old woman and I quit my job. I should note, it was an awesome job.

The Cincinnati Zoo & Botanical Garden was ranked number one in the country. This honor was not only because of a famous hippopotamus named Fiona. It was also because our team was innovative, creative, willing-to-fail, willing-to-get up and try again. We were a powerhouse. Our innovations within animal habitats and botanical beauty brought sustainability, conservation, community engagement, and investment to levels beyond our wildest imaginings.[1-6]

The zoo was a wickedly fun place to work. During my first week, I sat in my office giggling as the calls of gibbons interrupted my thoughts. I especially remember the sense of confusion I felt the first time I heard an elephant trumpet. Being born and bred in the Midwest, my brain took a moment to register that the noises in my immediate vicinity could be coming from elephants, of all things. I popped my head into my colleague's office to ask, *"Did you hear that?"* Her eyes lit up as a grin spread across her face. She was vicariously re-experiencing her own first time in my shoes.

The job encouraged walks throughout the campus. I would often meander across the zoo to sit with the manatees. From the childhood moment I encountered these gentle giants in the wild on the docks near my grandparent's condo in Florida, they became my immediate and enduring favorite animal. Our facility at the zoo was one of only two manatee rehabilitation sanctuaries in the country outside of Florida.[7] As an employee, I could visit whenever I wanted.

While manatees fill me with peace, joy, and love, birds are the exact opposite. They elicit stress, chaos, and fear. The roots run deep. I was fourteen when a bird found its way into our house through a disconnected dryer vent. It ended up in my bedroom as I was slowly waking from a restful sleep. Even today, the sound of its wings flapping around my head is real and immediate. Birds simply terrify me. The unpredictable swooping! The pointy beaks! No thank you!

When my beloved colleagues at the zoo heard of my ornithophobia, they immediately created an opportunity for me to work with Bernard, the "sweet and loving vulture." The common grackle that terrorized me as teenager was bad enough. To this day, I can barely handle the flitty nature of sparrows. So, a *vulture*? I was a hard "No!" Absolutely not.

Yet, with ample encouragement and reassurance from colleagues, and some deep breaths to ground myself, I mustered the courage and accepted the invitation to help train Bernard. The goal was to expose him to people other than his trainers in preparation for his debut in the Wings of Wonder show. On a crisp February morning, Bernard swooped through the stadium seating to snatch a piece of dead mouse from a little tin in my hand. The animal enrichment went well – both times.

Being part of the zoo team was nothing short of magical. It was a lush oasis in the city's urban core, filled to the brim with exotic animals. Inspiration flowed freely. I would walk through the tulips, delighting in the awe of children as they had up-close encounters with African painted dogs, lions, giraffes, and flamingos. Even during the hot, sticky summer months, when kids are prone to arm-thrashing breakdowns, there was something magical about the place. It seemed to radiate imagination, creativity, and joy. The work was meaningful, moving, and fun. It stretched my limits, soothed my soul, and brought me great joy. Yet, I decided to quit. Although I had taken several calculated risks in my life, this was by far the most dramatic.

Perhaps we should go back to the beginning.

After earning my graduate degree, doors opened. I joined the United Way team in Cincinnati, Ohio. Though I had plenty of jobs before graduate school, this felt like starting a grown-up career for the first time. I was creating a home and community for myself. After a short tenure with United Way, I was courted by and invited to support an up-and-coming nonprofit. I had invested hours into my Covington, Kentucky community, and they took notice. I became a team of one. The board I reported directly to had a big vision: eradicating generational poverty in the region. It was a boost to my ego and bank account. And I was fully invested...for all of sixteen months.

There were challenges working alone. Meanwhile, my inner voice was struggling to get my attention. After some time, I finally noticed. Soon thereafter, I landed a position at a small nonprofit whose mission was to help people become the best version of themselves. During my interview, I equated fundraising to friend-raising. That resonated with the founder, who gave me a chance. The experience opened a new world to me. Those were full and fruitful years. The organization grew from five employees to over a dozen. We were a real, unified team, and I was growing as much personally as I was professionally. At thirty, I got married with the love and support of my colleagues.

After several years, I felt it was time to move along. The nudge from within was getting louder and more persistent. I stepped into a lifelong passion and joined The Alzheimer's Association of Greater Cincinnati. Aging, death, and dying with dignity is deeply meaningful to me. I learned so much there, like what it meant to be fiercely committed to a mission. I also learned how to engage and empower people to be part of the change so desperately needed in the world. I had never felt so creative, or so much like a leader among leaders. Lifelong friendships were created during this season of life. We honored one another's gifts, connected deeply, and asked for support when we needed it.

Then – you guessed it – I got antsy there, too. Sure, I had a few years under my belt, yet my lifelong commitment to community and systemic change shifted. My next desire was to roll up my sleeves and return to direct care work. Soon I found a gem of a job at a continuum-of-care community. I was working in the same universe of aging issues, but in a more immediate way. My title: Director of Mission Integration and Spiritual Care. For me, it could not get any better than focusing on mission and spiritual health.

However, if you are not aware, the healthcare system in the United States is broken, and especially so for the aging population. We did our best to foster person-centered care. I was even sent on an all-expenses-paid pilgrimage to Italy to connect with the teachings of saints who served the aging community. But we were working against an entire industry, one that is emphatically *not* person-centered. As a human who leads with empathy and thrives on serving others, it was soul-sucking and debilitating. Or at least that is what I allowed it to do to me. After only two years, I was exhausted and severely unhealthy. That is when I found my way to the Cincinnati Zoo.

I was born in the space between Generation X and millennial. Generational hair-splitting has deemed me a "xennial," which refers to a supposed micro-generation born between 1977 and 1985. Millennials are projected to have twelve jobs in their lifetime.

I had been with six organizations in a timespan that represented a third of my working years. With each new job, my tenure got shorter and shorter. It was the opposite of the societal norm.

My inner script sounded something like this:

This is not fulfilling me.
I want to try something else.
I am more interested in serving the aging population.
I love community and systemic-level change.
I need to be in the trenches to really make a difference.

And so on. There was always a reason to move on to the next thing.

Unbeknownst to me, I was approaching my midlife calm. I was getting closer to insights into my authentic truths, clarity about what I was avoiding, and self-trust. Jumping from one job to another was not a midlife crisis. Though it may have appeared to be chaotic, it was simply my unique path. My truth was bubbling up. I was acting from the drive towards real calm. Soon that inner knowing would drown out the societal expectations I had internalized throughout my life, willingly and consciously or not. My true inner voice had been getting louder and stronger all along. It caused me to shift until I arrived at a place where I could no longer see anything except the possibility of calm. And I wanted that calm desperately. I was willing to risk everything. So, without a plan, I quit my job.

It was the summer of 2020, and the world was deep into the pandemic. I had been invited to co-chair the zoo's reopening committee. It was an enormous challenge. The heavy investment of time and energy simultaneously invigorated and exhausted me. Losing so many colleagues from being closed for ten weeks created opportunities to pivot. That word was thrown around a lot in 2020. My pivot found me in the elephant house in the wee hours of the morning, scooping poop, stuffing bales of hay into feeders, and bathing four of the largest of all land mammals.

After that, I would return to my home office to put in an additional eight hours of effort. The smell of the elephant house followed me home. Despite everything, I grew to love the cozy hours spent surrounded by books, travel photographs, and the rich green walls of my study that gradually turned into a proper home office.

Before the pandemic, the room had sat, woefully under-utilized, for over ten years. During those years I told both myself and others that one day I would be a consultant, assisting organizations with strategy, leadership development, and fundraising. But it all seemed far-off, part of some impossibly enchanted time of life where I could function without a reliable salary or benefits. The freedom of a consulting position attracted me, and I felt confident that I would be successful. The clarity was always there. I told myself, however, I could not have that as a 42-year-old, single adult.

Then, one day, I was walking along the floodwall that separates Covington from Newport and it came to me. I was not intentionally searching or thinking or processing. I was not fretting about work or the future. I was simply walking. It was a happy addition to my daily routine, and a way to sort myself out from the seemingly endless onslaught of work. On that walk, a thought came from nowhere: be a life coach. Initially, it made me pause. Then a smile blossomed deep inside, flowed throughout me, and caused the corners of my lips to turn up. Yes! Again, the thought: be a life coach!

How had I never considered this before? When I began to float the idea around, those were the exact words my closest friends and family repeated back to me. For perhaps the first time, I was not seeking approval. It felt so aligned, grounded, inspired, and confident. So, I committed myself to long workdays of constructing a reopening plan for the zoo. After that, I invested additional hours into researching coaching and entrepreneurship. The momentum was powerful. It sustained me through long evening hours of training, strategizing, and mapping out a plan. All the while, my vision and intention were becoming clearer and clearer.

Then, suddenly, opportunities began appearing. I refinanced my home, secured a more affordable monthly mortgage, and got access to equity. I attended free virtual trainings with thought leaders in the world of coaching. And like so many other pandemic-stressed businesses, the zoo arrived at the difficult but prudent decision to have a second round of layoffs in the summer of 2020. They offered voluntary separation packages, and I took the opportunity to depart with as much grace as I could muster.

Just like that, I was on a path to pursue a long, lingering dream that had been incubating over the countless miles I walked during the fateful pandemic year. Little did I know, I was embarking upon my Midlife Calm.

This book dives into the concept of midlife crisis and puts forth an alternative option – midlife calm. There are stories woven throughout to illuminate crisis and calm. There are questions that invite you into a place of curiosity and self-alignment. Perhaps it is time for you to embrace your Midlife Calm!

two

Four decades into life, I am well-acquainted with the concept of midlife crisis. Like most people, I know the stereotypical examples. I have heard people close to me claim they are having a midlife crisis. Some are in genuine distress; others are poking fun at themselves. A few years ago, I got curious about the concept. Perhaps this curiosity was a foreshadowing of my own so-called midlife crisis. Mostly, what I wanted to know was, who said it was a crisis?

The quintessential example is the fifty-something year-old guy who goes out and buys a sports car. The murmurs from friends, family, and acquaintances start immediately: he's obviously having a midlife crisis!

But is he? Hear me out. Say the person in question has always been enthralled by cars, has the financial means, and makes an informed decision to purchase a sports car. How, exactly, does that qualify as a crisis? It strikes me as more of a lifelong dream being lived into reality. To that I say, enjoy the ride!

This basic question – who said it was a crisis – was less about who and more about why is it deemed a crisis? For two years, I nonchalantly looked for insights, ideas, and inspiration. The culmination of what I discovered felt radically important to share with the world.

As it turns out, Elliott Jaques, a Canadian physician and psychoanalyst, was the person who said it was a crisis in 1965. As cited in Wikipedia:

> "A midlife crisis is a transition of identity and self-confidence that can occur in middle-aged individuals, typically 45 to 65 years old. The phenomenon is described as a psychological crisis brought about by events that highlight a person's growing age, inevitable mortality, and possibly lack of accomplishments in life. This may produce feelings of intense depression, remorse, and high levels of anxiety, or the desire to achieve youthfulness, make drastic changes to their current lifestyle, or feel the wish to change past decisions and events." [8]

Jaques claimed that the crisis itself is sparked by two dual realizations: that life is halfway complete, and that death is not just something that happens to others. In other words, things get real and personal.[9] Interestingly, he suggested that the midlife crisis could either be a result of achieving everything one desired, yet not seeing the point of it all, or of not achieving enough. Jaques' definition of midlife was when one "reached maturity by overcoming our denial of death and human destructiveness."[10] Moving from youthful idealism to "contemplative pessimism" and "constructive resignation"[11] was the primary achievement of middle age according to Jaques.

Yet, the concept was far from new when Jaques coined the phrase.

The idea has been in conversation for centuries. In the late 1800s, followers of Sigmund Freud suggested that the thoughts of individuals in midlife were driven by fear of impending death.[12] Carl Jung offered a different perspective in the early 1900s.[13] He asserted that the period of midlife is critical to individualization, self-awareness, and self-actualization. Jung said the failure to integrate thinking, feeling, sensation, and intuition in the period of midlife was what could lead to confusion in one's life and goals.

Psychosocial theorist, Erik Erikson suggested that there are eight life stages of development, each of which have a conflicting idea that must be overcome in order to "become a confident, contributing member of society."[14] Stage seven, middle adulthood, offers the conflict of generativity versus stagnation. Erikson said this is the period when adults find their purpose and begin to understand the value of improving the lives of generations to come. Without these realizations, a person will experience stagnation and disconnection. Erikson asserted that the inevitable reckoning with mortality and the responsibility to make the world a better place creates the pressure – and crisis – of midlife.

Daniel Levinson built upon Erikson's theory.[15] Levinson's stage crisis view states that as a person progresses through the eras of life, various developmental tasks must be mastered.[16] These tasks allow for transition between the stages. The transition from early to middle adulthood is represented by a reappraisal of the past and modification for future, largely related to work and marital relations.[17] This reappraisal can stir up disappointment and disillusionment. Levinson said this was a necessary part of transitioning to middle adulthood.

With years of work to fuel Jaques' theory, subsequent authors published research that substantiated his idea of the midlife crisis. Barbara Fried, in *The Middle-Age Crisis*, deemed the crisis a "normal aspect of growth, as natural for those in their forties as teething is for a younger age group." In 1976, Gail Sheehy brought the idea firmly into the mainstream with *Passages: Predictable Crisis of Adult Life*, which was later deemed by a survey conducted for the Library of Congress to be a book that most influenced people's lives.[18]

The theory grew. The story grew.

By 1972, a US government task force warned businesses that midlife crisis may be the cause of an uptick in the death rate of men between thirty-five and forty.[19] Allegedly, professional white men most commonly fell victim to midlife crisis because they were on the journey of self-actualization. With additional awareness, the impact was certainly more pervasive than solely middle and upper class, white men.

Gender became a point of consideration in the discussion. Sheehy's research found that a midlife crisis tends to range from three to ten years in men and two to five years in women.[20] She also proposed midlife crisis was more likely to be caused by work related issues for men, whereas women were more likely to have a midlife crisis related to personal evaluation of their roles and relationships. The common thread, however, was the range of intense emotions experienced during a midlife crisis. Remorse, humiliation, longing, disconnection, a lack of or heightened sexuality, confusion, resentment, and discontent are often at the core of the midlife crisis for both men and women. The triggers may appear in relationships, vocation, financial status, physical changes, loss, and aging.

The conversation around midlife crisis has been significant for decades. Who does it impact? When does it occur? What happens during a midlife crisis? This catchy phrase has become a cultural touchstone. It has offered language around what some people experience in the middle phase of life.

It has also created additional questions. Does everyone have a midlife crisis? Does anticipating a midlife crisis heighten the risk of having one? What age is midlife? Is a midlife crisis self-proclaimed and diagnosed, or are there external measurables to qualify the experience?

In *Coming of Age in Samoa*, anthropologist Margaret Mead shared that Americans expect teenage girls to have an adolescent crisis. As a result, many American teenage girls proceed to have an adolescent crisis. Mead went on to say that Samoans do not expect their teenage girls to experience emotional upheaval. As a result, they do not. Could this be the case for midlife crisis as well?

Despite society embracing the concept, there is an abundance of research that indicates the phenomenon is not real or inevitable. Freund and Ritter's review of research found ample data to support the unraveling of the idea of midlife crisis.[21]

Schaie and Willis found much of the research conducted on midlife crisis has been data collected in one point in time.[22] The absence of longitudinal data collection limits the results of these studies. Additionally, study samples have often been small and nonrepresentative. Specifically, Jaques' theories were largely based on a historical analysis of artists and few clinical studies.[23] Levinson's work was based on white, male research participants.

Other research has found that midlife is frequently a period of personal and professional stability or peak performance. Ski Hunter and Martin Sundel deem this the "midlife mythology."[24] Their work revealed that midlife is a period less likely to be demarcated by heightened crisis experiences.

A study conducted in 1995 called "Midlife in the United States" (MIDUS) found that people in midlife are typically "pretty satisfied."[25] Overall, individuals in this phase of life are at peak earning potential professionally, healthy, and experiencing busy social lives. This same study found that less than twenty percent of Americans experienced something they would categorize as a midlife crisis.

A longitudinal study by Helson and Wink found an increase of confidence, comfort, and stability in women age 43 to 52.[26] This was accompanied by a decrease in dependency and self-criticism. Additionally, Costa, Herbst, McCrae, and Siegler found that Americans aged 41 to 50 became less self-conscious and neurotic with age.[27] Aldwin and Levenson concluded that for most men, midlife is a time of achievement and satisfaction.[28] Similarly, most women successfully navigate moments that would be thought to trigger crisis: menopause, children leaving the home, and caring for aging parents.

These and countless other studies found that the concept of midlife crisis is far more of a pop culture catch-phrase than a predestined experience.[29-31]

Which brings us back to my original question: who said it was a crisis, and more so why is it deemed a crisis? Why would altering your course, exploring a new endeavor, or pursuing something that makes you blissful be labeled a crisis?

What if, instead of embracing the cultural construct of the midlife crisis, we opened ourselves to the possibility of individuality and authenticity? What if we stepped away from harmful cultural norms in a healthy manner? What if we celebrated each individual as they mimic a caterpillar dissolving into the chrysalis to become a butterfly? Or a dandelion finding its way through a crack in the pavement and pushing into the light of the concrete jungle? Perhaps what society has called the midlife crisis actually points to an individual about to live an even more incredible, irresistible life! What becomes possible when we shift our perspective, even by one degree?

three

What does midlife crisis mean to you? This is the question I asked hundreds of individuals. I found there are as many responses to the question as there are humans. Despite their variety, some consistent themes emerge. Here are a few representative samples:

When you look at your life and realize you're not where you planned to be at middle age, and then frantically try to be young again. When you start over to reach your goal, rather than assessing if that is still your goal.

Reaching the stage in life where you begin to really feel your mortality and then react to that–sometimes inappropriately.

A midlife crisis is everything falling apart at once: health, relationships, friends, work, family. It feels like the whole world crashing down on you from every angle, and you don't know what to do.

A midlife crisis is both a feeling of 'not being good enough' and a reflection of where you've been, often accompanied by some depression and anxiety about what's next.

It's like a duck gliding along the surface but underneath, where no one can see, paddling furiously to stay afloat.

Midlife crisis is another word for ageism! This phrase is an easy way to contribute to ageism without really intending to.

Feeling uninterested or indifferent about life. Lacking a sense of direction or desire when the previous plan and blueprint is no longer working.

Lacking clarity, yet still making significant changes that impact your career, relationships, finances, home, etc. Being fear based. Playing safe or playing not to lose, instead of playing to win.

The moment when you look at your life and wonder, how did this happen? This was not where I envisioned myself. The crisis is when one refuses to accept that it is okay. Although life is probably different than what you planned, it is still good.

Hearing these responses, it is clear I am not the only one well-acquainted with the phrase. These sentiments paint the picture. The theme of midlife crisis is a period of significant and invasive difficulty.

Beyond impulsively purchasing sports cars, the examples of how a midlife crisis plays out are also bountiful. Below is what a few people shared when I asked what specific examples come to mind when they think of midlife crisis:

Moving to a new city, buying something ridiculous, taking up an outrageous hobby, or dating someone who's not a good fit.

Making a big purchase like a fancy car, boat, etc. Or the opposite - cleaning house and getting rid of everything.

Getting your body pierced, buying a Harley Davidson, making an uncharacteristic luxury purchase, getting a tattoo, doing things you or others perceive to be reckless, or getting a young girlfriend so you can pretend to be young by association. Dyeing your gray hair, eyebrows, and/or mustache. Getting a toupee or hair plugs. Wearing clothes that were obviously marketed to people thirty years younger than you. Breast implants, tummy tucks, liposuction.

Not having savings, not being sure what you want to do with your life, and rebuilding from scratch.

Do any of these sentiments capture how you describe a midlife crisis? Were you surprised or challenged by any of the portrayals? What is your definition and what examples do you use to depict a midlife crisis?

Now that we have several perspectives, hopefully including your own, let's start to unpack midlife crisis as a concept. To further explore the classic midlife crisis, I offer the following two scenarios:

Scenario One:

Man: I bought a red Porsche!
Friend: Oh? What did your partner say?
Friend (behind man's back): What do you think about him buying that sports car? Looks like someone's having a midlife crisis!

Scenario Two:

Man: I bought a red Porsche!
Friend: Oh, wow! What inspired this? Let's go for a ride!

The friend's response in scenario one reflects personal judgement. The friend jumps to conclusions without creating space to learn more. The purchase of a sports car has no impact on the friend, yet the friend reacts from the basis of his/her internalized cultural norms.

The response in scenario two leans into vision, intention, and curiosity. The friend is less concerned with the past (the car was purchased) and more interested in the present and future (enjoying the ride).

This is what it looks like to debunk the myth of midlife crisis. By placing a new perspective or interpretation on a familiar scenario, there is an opportunity to shift. The first step of shifting from a worn-out, misaligned cultural norm is to notice without judgement or comparison. Noticing is the experience of turning inward and offering attention to what thoughts are floating through your mind, and to how your body is responding. Noticing is not agreeing or disagreeing with the thoughts or feelings, it is simply awareness. No judgement. No comparison.

When I linger a couple moments and notice, I become curious

about my interpretations of commitments and choices. For example, when I make a large purchase, I look at the timing and my finances instead of wondering if a friend would make the same purchase. Or when I dye my hair, I am clear that my intention is to be playful and fun. I embrace that motivation rather than operating from an intention to fit in. When I quit my job without another one lined up, I considered all the details of the decision. Slowing down to notice allows me to be clear and genuine, versus being mired in the rat race where success, accomplishments, and looking good are rewarded. The brief pause invites me to notice whether I am afraid and playing small, or if I am standing in an abundance of opportunity and possibility.

Again, the key to noticing is to not judge or compare. I cannot stress this point enough. When we pause to neutrally notice, we invite awareness that allows us to soften the scolding and disrespectful voice. Pausing to notice quiets the voice that has adopted the tone and values of external forces that are at times unaligned with your own inner truth.

Dismantling your own harsh inner critic creates an opportunity to engage with others in a less rigid and judgmental fashion. Engaging with yourself and others from a place of vision, intention, and curiosity creates forward flow and momentum. A crisis does the opposite – it creates barriers and obstacles.

Without pausing to notice, it is easy to be unwittingly swept into a dilemma that exists within American culture. This dilemma is a fixation on success, accomplishment, continual building, and obtaining more and more, instead of individually calibrating ourselves. Self-calibration, or regulation, looks like assessing what is working for ourselves – our body, mind, and spirit – and proceeding with an individualized plan. If you calibrate only according to external influences – success, accomplishment, and obtaining more – you will inevitably create misalignment for yourself. It is common for this to manifest as a crisis – physically, mentally, emotionally, or spiritually.

A midlife crisis pulls you into a belief that you have not accomplished enough. Embracing the belief that you are right or wrong, good or bad, or need to be "more" of anything is a trap. These beliefs pull you away from your inner truth and unique path. They send you down a trail of conformity that may not align with who you are and your purpose in life. Anytime these beliefs are created, passed down, and adopted without pausing to examine whether they support you, a disservice is done.

The proliferation of believing I am right or wrong, good or bad, or need to be "more" of anything causes a robotic shift into human doing versus human being. When this happens, effort and energy are directed to the mechanics of life versus the intention. This results in exaggerated attention invested in the how, when, and what rather than why. This causes the focus to be largely outside of oneself, which creates misalignment.

Take for example the extreme pursuit of fitness. You may ask, how does this constitute a midlife crisis? Well, I know a woman who began cycling when she turned fifty. She claimed that she only ate for the purpose of nutrition. First, she became strong and muscular. Then she got lean. Eventually, she started to appear unhealthy. With every passing week she biked longer and longer distances, with increasing intensity, until her body arrived at a breaking point. She was rushed to the hospital after collapsing during a morning ride. Tests indicated she had developed an abnormal heartbeat and damage to her heart tissue. The commitment that began as an admirable pursuit of health quickly turned to a dangerous obsession. I am happy to share that she has now created a plan, with the support of her cardiologist, that empowers her to live a life aligned with fitness and wellbeing.

Being healthy is an intention. The **why** may support longevity, mobility, legacy, or a number of other motivations. Cycling is a mechanic. It is one option to support the overall intention of being healthy. Other mechanics include drinking water, clean eating, and getting ample sleep. These answer the questions of **what** to do and **how** to be healthy. When attention shifts disproportionately to the mechanics the intention becomes lost. When intention is lost, we devolve into human doings versus human beings. We become lost.

Doing versus being is an easy trance to be lured into. I know from experience. When I have a ton of tasks at work and home, my body literally turns rigid. My shoulders pinch up, my neck and throat get tight, and at times I feel an internal jumpiness. The thoughts running through my mind are often scolding, bossy, and disrespectful:

It doesn't matter how you feel, get it done!
Everyone else can do it, what's wrong with you?
I don't care if you're tired or strained, you have to do this for work.

This is not how I was when I was a child. I did not grow up in an environment of demeaning language and excessively rigorous expectations. And yet, at some point, I became enthralled with the mechanics – the doing. I told myself that what I accomplished and contributed was more important than who I was. Perhaps this is because the mechanics of life are transactional and therefore easily measured, embraced, and celebrated. I was hungry to be embraced and celebrated. So, this inner talk tract became the message and tone that played out for far too long. It fed into the progression of career successes I enjoyed with amplified titles, increased pay, and heightened responsibility and accolades. Yet I was never deeply satisfied. The trance of human doing pulled me away from myself. I was stuck in the hamster wheel of accomplishment and success. Meanwhile, I was searching for anything to satisfy my desire to be aligned with my true self – my desire for calm.

For years, I pushed through physical and mental resistance in the work setting and somehow mustered whatever was necessary to complete various assignments in excellence. For me, completing in excellence meant being on time, every consideration accounted for, a thorough plan for roll out of the project, measurable results accomplished, and active evaluation to keep the work relevant. Pushing through my physical and mental resistance was celebrated and rewarded in the professional world. During those years of life, I would often arrive home and immediately take a nap. Time that could have been allocated for me to focus on personal needs and wants was not leveraged. Napping was my way to tap out, shut down, check out. I often experienced myself as uptight, stressed, and misaligned. I was anything but calm.

That was my vicious cycle. Despite the warning signs and rumble strips, I gave all my effort, energy, and attention to the parts of life that were outwardly measured and rewarded. I was depleted when it came time to focus on me, family, friends, or my community. Although counter intuitive, I continued in this way until I arrived at a breaking point. Some call this a midlife crisis. I call it clarity. I call it my midlife calm.

Quitting a job without another lined up is one example of what some would deem a midlife crisis. There are countless ways this phenomenon could play out. A few additional examples are:

Getting a facelift and tummy tuck, dying hair, extreme pursuit of fitness…

Having an affair with a younger woman or man, ending a marriage, purchasing a sports car…

Returning to school to pursue a different career path, beginning or ceasing going to church, extended long-distance travel.

I invite you to take a deep breath and give yourself a moment. Really notice yourself right now. Reread the list of how a midlife crisis may manifest. As you read through the examples, what do you notice? Do you find yourself affirmatively nodding that these are indeed examples of midlife crises? Do you immediately conjure additional examples and create an even more robust list? Or do you resist and find yourself responding: *"Most of these are on point. But returning to school to pursue a different career path is definitely not a midlife crisis. It's courageous!"*

Are you grounded in intention or mechanics? Are you showing up as a human doing or a human being? I invite you to notice yourself without judgement.

four

In Chapter Two, we reviewed how the term midlife crisis came into existence. In Chapter Three we looked at how this phenomenon can manifest in everyday life. Prior to fully unveiling the concept of midlife calm, let's explore the power of language, labels, and stories as it pertains to creating either crisis or calm. The fact is, humans are meaning making machines. Much of what we believe originates with our words.

I'll begin with a quote from Gandhi.

> *"Your beliefs become your thoughts,*
> *Your thoughts become your words,*
> *Your words become your actions,*
> *Your actions become your habits,*
> *Your habits become your values,*
> *Your values become your destiny."*

Gandhi's thread starts with our beliefs and ends with our destiny. That means that your beliefs point directly to your destiny. The profound wisdom of this message deserves to be broken down and digested, as we explore the concept of midlife crisis.

I appreciate being grounded with the definition of words. The first two words of Gandhi's quote are:

Belief: An acceptance that a statement is true or that something exists.[32]

Thought: An idea or opinion produced by thinking, or occurring suddenly in the mind.[33]

I frequently substitute the word 'story' for 'thought'. As an idea or opinion is produced or suddenly pops in my mind, I experience the story of my life. Allow me to illustrate this idea.

During my sophomore year of college, I had a paper due for my theology class. The topic escapes me, but it was heavily factored in the final grade. Although I considered myself a diligent student, I was still getting the hang of time management and completing tasks in excellence. It was around nine in the evening when I arrived in the computer lab – eleven hours before the deadline. My intention was to camp out and crank through the night, get a little sleep, and be at least somewhat ready to show up for class at eight the next morning.

I found it easier to think when not sandwiched between two other students, so I always sought out a computer at the end of the long lab tables. When I arrived, I could see my usual territory occupied. The place was packed. My stomach sank as my eyes darted across the room in search of a free computer. One remained, thank goodness. I bee-lined across the room to snag it before any rivals could do the same. Time was of the essence.

After ritualistically unpacking all the necessary amenities – textbook, notebook, bottle of water, highlighter, stress ball – I reached under the table to turn the computer on. I waited the ninety seconds required in 1998 for it to boot up. Nothing happened. Maybe someone had turned the monitor off? I pushed that button, too. Nothing. I frantically scanned the room for another available spot. My fellow students were heads down, headphones in, furiously completing their own assignments, oblivious to my plight. With increasing desperation, I indiscriminately pushed every button all over again, then frantically wiggled the cords at the back of the computer. I was pissed. How could this college, which I paid so much money to attend, have such crappy computers for their students? Why didn't the tech team check these computers before finals week? This was not the time for them to be on the fritz!

My anger turned to panic. This was a *crisis*! I suddenly realized how tired I was. I felt myself spiraling downward. I pondered having to wait for an available computer before even *beginning* my paper. This would set things back. I may not get any sleep at all. I fruitlessly tried the buttons a third time. I started praying to just please get this machine up and running. Still, nothing. I began to assess the status of every other person in the lab, hoping to see someone packing up to leave. Maybe that girl over there was close to finished; she seemed to be at the end of her rope.

Ten minutes passed. I started to strategize how I would ask my professor for an extension. Email was out, since I had no computer to write one on. It was too late to call. My stomach was in knots and my chest was tight. I felt defeated. My shoulders slumped. I wanted to cry. This was it. I would fail the class. My mind was in a frenzy, yet my body was lethargic. I felt paralyzed. I sat and watched the hands of the clock on the wall climb all the way to ten pm, spiraling internally all the while. I somehow felt lost, urgent, and apathetic all at the same time.

Then, as I cast my eyes downward, I noticed something curious. Lying next to the power strip was an unplugged cord. Could this be the solution? I crawled under the table to firmly plug it in, oblivious to the sideways glances from the people on my right and left. They had not noticed me sitting blankly before a comatose computer for the entire past hour. Now I was back to pushing buttons. Computer: check. Monitor: check. The screen glowed, then, after another sixty obligatory seconds, the computer churned to life. I was winning again! I was back in business! I was ready to write this paper like nobody's business!

For that hour, I lived in my own self-perpetuated crisis because I believed the computer was dead. My mind immediately determined this was a crisis. The stories played out in my thoughts instantly – a failing grade or at best a late submission. The computer was simply unplugged.

Sure, my assignment was minor in the grand scheme of things. But does it matter? Look what it did to my mind and body. The story was that the only computer available to me was dead. Just like that, I too was dead. I believed I was in crisis. In no time, my beliefs became my thoughts, my thoughts became my words, and my words became my actions. My internal language sent me down the path of defeat. Then I proceeded to act out my beliefs for an entire hour. It was a crisis because I believed it, thought it, and spoke it to myself. This is true in major as well as minor moments of life – including, I propose, those moments we deem as midlife crisis.

We are a society of stories. Some are happy and playful; others are very much the opposite. Some are factual, others are lies. Either way stories are told and believed. They come forward in our words and then actions, and they continue to evolve. That is how stories work. They are incredibly powerful. And what is behind stories? We are!

This means that you and I, as the story tellers, are incredibly powerful.

What if your midlife crisis was a story, an idea or opinion produced by thought? As you keep a corner of your mind open to that idea, allow me to share a few more stories.

Story One:

Once there was a little girl. She had pale skin and stick-straight, dark brown hair. She excelled in school and had a heart that yearned to include everyone. At a young age, she longed to be liked, loved, and accepted for who she was. This little girl took it upon herself to lead when her friends were floundering, but at school she did not feel confident or cool enough to succeed as a leader on the social front. Teachers and peers crowned her with the label: "A good student. A kind friend." The little girl was incredibly proud.

The good student and kind friend grew up living into a story that became her reality. She was a good student throughout college, a quick study in her career, and excelled in all the tasks handed to her. She was deeply loyal. She kept her radar tuned into others throughout life. When they floundered, she showed up to offer encouragement and support.

She married a man with several addictions. In her kindness, she enabled others, including him. She overcompensated by giving outwardly, even when inwardly she felt lacking. She leaned so far into the label of "good and kind" that she forgot about herself. When she felt sad, she shoved it down. When she was angry, she forced herself to process and diffuse the feelings, all without burdening anyone else.

Decades into her life, as the little girl became a woman, she had to dig into her story and the role she was playing in her own life. She had to get honest about her needs. She was still innately the same. She still yearned to include everyone. Eventually, she realized she got to be included too – she is part of everyone.

Some stories look like fairy tales from the outside, but there is almost always more. This is especially the case if the story is focused on just one aspect of a person's life. I have yet to meet a human with a small or narrow story. And when what is presented is small or narrow, the story is almost always incomplete. Have the stories you have heard or lived related to midlife crisis been small or narrow?

By the way, that little girl is now living an abundant, juicy, energized life. She is me.

Story Two:

The eighty-seven year-old father of four and grandfather of ten had previously commanded any room with his six-foot-plus stature and complimentary build. Up until a year ago, he lived alone, mowed his yard, made his meals, and drove to church and the senior center every week to pray, share a meal, and play cards.

Gradually, he started to change. His yard became unkempt. He started noticeably losing weight. He became scared to drive, even the well-worn three-mile trip to church. His neighbors, with good intentions, began whispering to one another. *"He seems to be slipping. Maybe senility's setting in?"*

Early on, this was a story of not knowing. As decades passed, this became a story of naming something inaccurately. Stories layered on stories. If what was known was communicated, it would become real. Yet, it already was real. This is the story of Alzheimer's disease. It came into focus over a century ago, in 1906, when the disease was discovered and named. Yet, for decades following the discovery, whenever a person experienced unexplainable cognitive decline, it was still called hardening of the arteries or senility. Even today it still goes unnamed.

It takes time for medical professionals to wrap their heads around a new, complicated disease – especially when, up until recently, it could not be diagnosed with one hundred percent accuracy without a postmortem brain autopsy. As laypeople learned of this disease, there was a significant fear factor involved in believing that a mother, father, or partner could live with such a horrible, incurable disease.

Whether discussed or not, diseases are real. The impacts of not telling the story of Alzheimer's disease – leaving it undiagnosed, not getting clear on what it means and what's to come – are detrimental. Avoidance represents fear. Often communication, connection, clarity, and a way forward are created by shedding light on situations that feel uncomfortable or scary.

Today, fifty-five million individuals are living with Alzheimer's disease worldwide and there are nearly ten million new cases per year.[34] When we sugar-coat or refuse to tell the story, we all suffer. Families and support circles of those living with Alzheimer's negotiate personal and professional time, fight the healthcare system, and often lose themselves in the process of caregiving. For well over a century, this story has been avoided or represented through muted versions.

Some stories look like tragedy. Those are often the ones we chose not to tell. Sadly, not telling the story, or not being fully truthful with the story, does not make things any better. When we shed light on the whole story – the honest story – that is when we arrive at healthier individuals, families, and communities. What story are you avoiding telling? Have you muted part of your life by telling the story that you are in a midlife crisis? How does this serve you, your family, your community?

Story Three:

Charlie had olive skin and stood just shy of three feet tall. In fourth grade a boy decided to point out that Charlie wasn't white or black. He poked fun at his differences and got other kids to join him in the laughter. Like wildfire, the joking became harassment. It was cutting and intended to make Charlie feel excluded and disliked. It worked.

Charlie searched for any support from others. He thought maybe the girls would be more forgiving of his differences. His little sister was always kind when they played together. But even the girls backed away. They did not join in with the ringleader, but they and many other classmates shrank away, trying to remove themselves from a situation that felt so painful, hateful, and confusing.

Charlie mustered his mental strength to endure for as long as he could. He did not tell his parents he was being bullied; he didn't want them to worry. He was mostly able to keep his grades up, with only the occasional dip. When his parents lovingly asked about a low score, he brushed it off as having a bad day. He never talked to anyone about the bullying. Day by day, year by year, Charlie continued to suffer. Finally, he could no longer take the cutting words, the shoves in the hallway, the pointed fingers, or the laughing. He was worn down and he ended his life.

Charlie is labeled the victim in this story. The classmates who harassed him were the bullies. And then there is everyone else: the bystanders who looked away and failed to speak up and offer support. Bullying is rampant in our society, as is suicide. It is the result of many dynamics, including lack of supportive resources and low or nonexistent self-worth.

Yet, by labeling a person as a victim, we deem them to be helpless. And by labeling a person as a bully, we create an identity that they adopt and live into. Our words become our actions. When I am called a victim or a bully, my actions are likely to align. It is this way with all words. The more I am called courageous, the more courageous I become. The more I am called timid, the more timid I become.

Just as it is important to flip the script and use language such as "a person living with Alzheimer's Disease" or "a woman beating cancer" instead of "Alzheimer's patient" or "cancer patient," it is important to become person-centered in all arenas of life. It is a more formidable obstacle to completely rebirth oneself out of their label. Person-centered renaming also creates clarity. The language developed in *Peace Be With You: Christ-Centered Bullying Solution*, by Frank Dilallo and Thom Powers supports this shift.[35] Instead of calling someone a "bully," the language is a "person who mistreats." Bullying can be physical, emotional, and mental; therefore, to call someone a bully leaves a lot up for interpretation. This shift in language creates an opportunity for a person to discontinue the mistreatment.

In a similar way, instead of "victim," Dilallo and Powers speak of a "person who is mistreated". With this language, the person is no longer helpless. It creates room to step into possibilities and puts the person who is mistreated in a position where s/he can do something. They become a moving target, and more difficult to mistreat.

Finally, the label of "bystander" is passive. This changes to a "person who witnesses." They are not the aggressor, nor the one toward whom the aggression is directed. Witnesses play a vital role. Language invites the person witnessing to consider whether they are being passive or throwing fuel on the fire.

Society has crafted some cunning tricks through the stories we tell, believe, and act out. On one hand, we are told to be our own unique individuals, to stand out, and speak our truth. On the other hand, we are expected to do what we are told, not to ask questions, and to conform in acceptable ways. These messages are conflicting and confusing. The dichotomy of being real or "acceptable" is baked into humans through the stories we tell and the language we use. When have you been labeled and how has that served you? Have you deemed yourself or another to be in a midlife crisis? How does this language shape your life?

Stories are powerful. As are you and I.

Stories shape our lives. They shape whether you are destined to a life of crisis or calm. So, I invite you to pause for ten minutes and reflect on the following questions.

What story are you telling?

What story are you believing?

What story are you embodying?

In Gandhi's thread, the second and third statements in the cascade are *"your thoughts become your words"* and *"your words become your actions."* This invites us to notice the words we use and to be honest about the actions they evoke. Language is a significant part of how the concept of midlife crisis is constructed.

Let me ask you a question: How do you feel when someone says, *"You have to _____."* Fill in the blank with anything: make dinner, fold the clothes, create a spreadsheet, attend a meeting.

I tend to feel resistant. When I hear a "have to" statement, I consider who is issuing the command, make a judgement regarding their impact on my life, and then choose to either reveal my resistance or swallow my pride and do what I have been told do. Can you relate?

What about when someone says, *"You should _____."* Again, it could be anything: put gas in the tank, wash that pair of jeans, make ten sales calls, build your client pipeline.

I tend to receive this as a judgement, as if the speaker knows better than me. It seems bossy, directive, controlling. It does not feel good to be controlled. It is easy to spiral into believing maybe they do know more than me, and I should do that thing they told me to do, but less from a learning and curiosity perspective, and more from a place of self-doubt. Suddenly, I have become small and resistant. What else does "you should" elicit within you?

Now, what if someone says, *"I wish you would _____"*: communicate, pay attention, or be less selfish?

This one is a blend of ugly feelings. It too confers its own connotations of holier-than-thou judgement and provokes that same old resistance. I defensively deflect, making an instant list of the things I wish they would do or be.

One final example. What about when a person says, *"If only you _____."* Were smarter, skinnier, more generous with your time, detail-oriented?

Now I feel disappointed in myself and possibly also the person speaking. They are focused on what they perceive as my deficiencies. The seed has been planted. I question whether I could or should be something different. It goes well beyond the healthy approach of noticing, choosing, and accepting feedback. I unconsciously create a story about how I could be stronger, prettier, better. I disconnect from myself and allow this person's feedback to become my north star, even if it is actually just a fading flame.

The deeper question is this: What happens when the person saying *"You have to…you should…I wish…or if only…"* is you? Let that land. How often are you creating resistance, self-doubt, and judgement of and within yourself?

This matters in the quest to creating an alternative to midlife crisis because language evokes powerful feelings and responses. If you or I deem ourselves or another to be in a midlife crisis, we will likely feel remorse, depression, anxiety, and regret. The word crisis elicits these reactions, just as being told I have to do something elicits a different set of reactions. Each of us has a choice. You can intentionally choose words that support yourself and others, or you can be enslaved by the feelings and responses that flow from unintentional language. Words, inflections, tone, and nonverbals all comprise the power of language. Language can set us up for excellence, mediocrity, or failure.

Another layer of our language comes in the form of labels. Labeling communicates information about someone or something using a short word or phrase with a strong meaning. Labels are powerful and dangerous. They are the mechanism used to simplify and categorize. Labels often relate to judgements, and as a result they can create stigma, fear, bias, stereotypes, hearsay, and an inability to interact with someone as a person instead of their label.

It is no secret that we are a species of isms: racism, sexism, classism, ableism, and ageism, just to name a few. Every time we accept the language, inferences, and microaggressions that validate any ism, we are saying it is acceptable, whether explicitly or not. Ageism particularly haunts the concept of midlife crisis. Though subtle, there is a sense within Western culture that life begins falling apart as early as a person's forties and certainly fifties, denoting a gradual decline and insignificance that lingers throughout the remainder of one's life. This decrescendo indirectly elevates youth. To embrace the concept of midlife crisis, is to unwittingly let toxic societal beliefs conquer our thoughts, words, habits, values, and even destinies.

These days, I am intimately connected to the language I practice. I also notice the language around me. Here are some examples of language I encounter in everyday life:

Plus-Size Model: The plus-size models depicted in media are often size fourteen or more. Size fourteen typically equates to "extra-large" in clothing. Interestingly, the typical American woman in 2022 has measurements that fit clothing sizes ranging from fourteen to eighteen.[36] Why has our society labeled a typical size woman as "plus size?" The greater point, isn't a model a model, whether she wears size two or twenty-two? The label becomes the focus, which prevents us from interacting with the person.

Failure: Thomas Edison famously had one thousand failed attempts before inventing the light bulb.[37] Yet Edison did not call these failures. Rather, he considered each a lesson in the larger journey of his ultimate discovery. When one labels something a failure, it is reduced to rubbish, which often creates a stall or halt. When one deems a failure to be a lesson, it is considered valuable, and one can keep moving proactively forward.

Retarded: In the late 1800s, this term was used for individuals with intellectual disabilities. Although it was meant to communicate specifically within the realms of education and personal care needs, the word quickly devolved into a way to demean others. For over sixty years, the hurtful impact of this word remains. Language can be a weapon. It is always imperative to know when you are wielding a weapon.

The Terrible Twos: Many friends with children have shared their dread of the "terrible twos," only to realize that age three or four were far more challenging in their child's development. The label created needless anxiety. As stated earlier, humans are meaning making machines. We find what we are looking for. If you seek evidence of the terrible twos, you will likely find it. Removing the label and embracing the seasons of early childhood could establish a more positive experience for families.

Do these examples heighten your awareness of the language you encounter or use every day? Does the language you use limit or serve you? What would change if you shifted your language? Take some time to notice the language you have become accustomed to. Get curious.

Once you have connected with your language, return to a time your language elicited fear, confusion, and scarcity. Did you enjoy those moments? Looking back, how could you have leveraged language to empower yourself?

These are important seeds to plant. Being aware of your language will support you in unearthing any existing or foreboding midlife crisis. Allow your language to be a tool used to shift from crisis to calm.

Finally, stressors are important to acknowledge as we assess the concept of midlife crisis. People encounter stressors every day: work responsibilities, home upkeep, tending to relationships, managing finances, the list is endless. With each passing year we are more prone to the loss of loved ones, professional setbacks, and shifts in health and physical ability. These realities can pile up and be experienced as a crisis, however, it may be more accurate to call it an overload. Overload is common when playing multiple roles in life – spouse, parent, employee, neighbor, and more. These roles are intertwined with the doing-ness of life – the mechanics and responsibilities. They can become heavy and burdensome, hence the word stressors.

Studies show that lower education and scarcity of resources correlates to more intense stressors during midlife.[38] It is important to recognize that as we do our inner work, there are very real external factors that impact the unique life paths of every individual. That is not to say stressors are not present in every phase of life for a variety of people. Yet, recall my "crisis" situation in the computer lab. This was a stressor, not a full-blown crisis.

Stressors can also be positive. Consider the first cry of a newborn. This initial wail is an important step of introducing their lungs to life outside the womb. It is the first transition of many in life. A baby leaves the cozy, warm, snug environment of their mother's womb to be thrust into a cold, bright, and utterly foreign space. A stressor, to say the least! When the baby is swaddled and rocked, some sense of safety returns through an emulation of what they knew so well. Birth is not typically deemed a crisis to the families who embrace the child, nor is it nonchalantly identified as a stressor. Yet birth sets the stage for a journey with seasons which are accompanied by inherently stress laden transitions. It is through stress that we stretch, learn, and grow. My dad refers to the gold in every situation. Even through the stress of radical change, there are gifts and gold to be found in every moment.

Some cultures are more sensitive to the phenomenon of midlife crisis than others. This begs the question: is midlife crisis a cultural construct? Could it be that the culture of youth within Western societies perpetuate these stressors, and through language and labeling we create what's now called the midlife crisis for ourselves?

My invitation is for each of us to do the personal work of pausing to notice, then shifting and sculpting our thoughts, words, and actions in ways that celebrate differences and commonalities. To be a healed community, we get to be healed individuals who practice intentional language. To shift from lives where crisis is a fear, we get to be people who embrace calm in our beliefs, thoughts, words, actions, habits, and values.

five

I have always loved to dance. Not necessarily ballet, ballroom, swing, or square dancing, though I have offered my own renditions of each from time to time. My kind of dancing is free form. It usually starts with toe tapping, then organically moves throughout my body, and launches into full-body interpretive dance without notice. My arms in the air waving from here to there. My hips gyrating and my butt popping (when necessary, according to the music of course). And my face…my face does all the things – expressing attitude, cracking up in sheer self-entertainment, and lip syncing.

Dancing has always been a healthy release. Like sports, dance improves heart and lung function, endurance, motor fitness, and muscular strength. It increases coordination, balance, flexibility, and bone strength. Beyond the physical benefits, as little as five minutes of dancing also increases cognitive function.[39] The endorphins released in those mere five minutes can boost happiness and improve creative thinking patterns.[40]

As a child, my first attempts at dancing took the form of running through our long, narrow plot of land with my arms outstretched like a bird in flight. Movement brought me to a place where my inner fire burned bright. Dance offers the freedom to be goofy, confident, and crazy.

Throughout childhood, dance often took the form of two-person performances. My older sister and I would create magical mini productions as date night entertainment for my parents. One special evening, we created a dinner and show.

Preparation was serious business. We tore into a hope chest of prom dresses, scarves, and shoes outgrown by our aunts, formally set a folding table with a tablecloth and fine silver, and sifted through a stack of records for the perfect musical accompaniment. We ultimately settled on a Mickey Mouse record, my personal favorite. Then, we fully choreographed every song.

The show began after my parents finished the five-star meal of instant spaghetti we prepared. Despite the absence of any outward laughter, there is no way our mom and dad didn't wonder when it would end. Instead, they clapped at the right times and waited patiently during wardrobe changes between songs. It was not only fun, but our heartfelt gift to them.

At some point in my transformation into a teenager, I became rigid and self-conscious. I doubted whether I was any good and felt certain that I would look silly. I do not remember dancing between fifth and eighth grades. Middle school was hard. I was chubby and covered with cystic acne. This lethal combination made me withdraw in a culture that celebrates the thin and perfectly-complected. The flow and freedom of showing up as my true self was stifled in more ways than just dance. I was navigating my way into what I deemed to be acceptable. My internal talk included a lot of *"I should be this way"* and *"If only I was that way."*

Fortunately, I grew up in a home where I was free to share my insecurities. My dad loved and celebrated every curve of my mom's body. My mom genuinely loved and embraced me. They held me as I cried about believing other girls were prettier and that I was missing out on young love. Though my family honored inner and outer beauty of all kinds, I mostly felt awkward and incomplete as a teen. I was committed to locking the free-spirited little girl away in order to measure up to external norms and pressures.

When the time came, I chose to attend a new high school without any of my previous classmates. It was intimidating and exhilarating, and an opportunity to step away from years of painful middle school experiences.

This is how I found myself in the bleachers of Central Catholic High School during a freshman class mixer. I attended with the encouragement of my parents and older sister, knowing that it was the perfect way to meet my new classmates. I think my heart knew it was a good choice, too.

I sat in the stands glancing down at the basketball court, which had been transformed into a dance floor. Everyone had gathered in circles, laughing, connecting, and dancing to the pop hits they seemed to know instinctively. Though I was not hip enough to know the songs, the desire to join in the dance swelled within me. As much as I tried to focus on making small talk in the bleachers, the fun, connectivity, and freedom available on the dance floor lured me.

I just didn't know how to throw myself into it. Which circle would most readily welcome me? How would I move my body without looking ridiculous? What if a slow song came on? That last one was particularly terrifying. I would never expect a boy to dance with me!

Without conscious thought, I found myself, as if in slow motion, skipping down the wooden bleachers and onto the dance floor, hurtling towards a very good or very poor decision. A song I loved came on. Then I spotted Samantha, a girl from my side of town. She motioned for me to join her circle. Yes! This was my opportunity! I could not have been any happier. She was beautiful, fun, popular, and a great dancer, too.

Crazed teenage body-thrashing ensued. Our circle burst open. The music moved me to bridge the open space between our dance bubble and another nearby. We playfully egged each other on. By the end of the night, I was dripping with sweat from the nape of my neck to the small of my back. The floor was packed and we were a bunch of happy soon-to-be freshman.

The flame within me that had almost gone out during middle school had been reignited. Ever since that freshman mixer in Toledo, Ohio, the flame has continued a steady burn. There have been moments when it felt tiny, but I have learned that as long as we are alive, our inner fires can never be fully extinguished. The little girl or little boy within each of us is ever present, ready to run through a plot of land with arms outstretched like a bird. Ready for you to reunite with the freedom of goofiness and confidence. The rigidity that accumulates as we age comes from adopting external expectations without checking in to see if what we are adopting aligns with who we are. The hesitation comes from putting on masks to protect ourselves when we feel hurt, embarrassed, and afraid.

I was not the best dancer on the gymnasium floor that night. Nor am I to this day. That is the point! Relinquishing the labels of good, better, or great regarding my dancing skills is what supported me in realigning with my true self. Breaking free of the story that I was not a good dancer was a step in the direction of casting off the masks I wore during middle school to protect myself. I was the permission for others to join the dance floor that night. I continue to be that permission every time I dance, sing, and literally just show up as myself.

There are many songs that talk about the fire within: how we shy away from it, how it can be intimidating or negative, and how we can empower it. The fire within is a beacon of light guiding us home. It allows us to find our authentic selves while casting a warm light out into the world. But it starts from within.

I agree with what Garth Brooks said in his song "Standing Outside the Fire." A life merely survived is not what you and I are after. Nor is a life based on the expectations of others. To burn bright, I stoke my fire by pursuing adventure, loving other humans, speaking my truth, and always joining in on the dance party. What causes your inner fire to burn bright?

six

"There is more to life than increasing its speed."

Mahatma Gandhi

Western culture comes with a range of spoken and unspoken expectations. Typically, those expectations go something like this:

You are born. You create connections and community, often through sports, music, church, and your neighbors. You arrive at school and learn that you are required to sit and focus, even when you feel antsy. You do your best. Everything is ranked. First, stickers and gold stars, next, medals and trophies, and then, grades from A to F. You notice an A feels better. When you earn an A you decide that you are good, valuable, and worthy. Conversely, when you earn an F, you decide that you are bad, undeserving, and you may shrink back.

Many finish twelve years of school. You proceed to trade school, college, or a job. In the eyes of society, you are an adult. With that comes the expectation of a job that pays your bills and rent. Life is full of excitement and pressure. You are committed to excelling. You pursue money and relationships. You keep working hard. You are diligent. You notice what works and what does not, and you strive to climb the professional ladder.

Perhaps you connect with another person and see the possibility of a life together. This is the person who will be there for you through thick and thin. You start building together. A bigger house with a yard near a good school district for your children. Maybe a pet. You strive to be a good neighbor.

Your work hours and responsibilities grow. After some time, you are amazed at what you have accomplished in three or four decades of life. You also feel the weight of it all. You notice how heavily your time and energy are invested in your work, which pays for the life you want. Any additional energy you have is committed to the necessities: grocery shopping, laundry, paying bills, walking the dog, shuttling the kids to practices.

Often, without realizing it, you become less connected to your partner than ever before. Maybe work becomes an energy-sucking burden, rather than a vehicle to help you live the life you want to live. Sometimes, you can't even remember what that life looks like.

But there are several decades left to live.

This, for better or worse, is the story of too many. It is also the way of our brains: we dig ruts for ourselves, and we settle deeper into them day by day.[41] These ruts are part of our brain's functioning to allow for a degree of efficiency and ease. In that space of efficiency and ease, it is easy to be swept into the cultural norm of success, building wealth, climbing the career ladder, having a home with a yard, and two and a half kids. To be clear, this life is not necessarily bad. It may, however, often be achieved in a bit of a trance.

Here is a version of how the rest of the story goes:

A day comes – or several – where you notice a nagging feeling from within. Although you attempt to ignore it and remain on the course you have set for yourself, a thought continually creeps up. Finally, it is so persistent and loud that you must listen. It makes you question the life you are living. Suddenly, you want to get off the hamster wheel of life. You have invested years in a fast-paced, success-first approach. You finally realize the extent to which this has left you feeling flat, exhausted, and unfulfilled.

You re-commit to paying attention to yourself, to adding your own twist to life. With consistent investment, you create a whole new way of thinking. Perhaps your job is not at all what you truly want to be doing. Perhaps you are aching to travel. Perhaps you are willing to take that leap into dating, or buy a boat, or take singing lessons, or adopt a puppy, or buy a sports car, or recommit to your partner, or pursue a second language.

So, you do. You feel like you can exhale. And for the first time in what has probably been a very long-time, you can breathe deeply. You also feel awkward because you are not completely sure if it is 'right' or 'good' to reprioritize your life. Doubts arise. There may be questions:

What if I let others down?
Will people think I've lost my mind?
Can I feel this good and still accomplish what needs to be done?

Direct answers to those questions will not arrive immediately. Yet you will experience profound freedom if you commit to being curious, listening to your inner voice and shifting. Eventually, you will feel more yourself than ever before. You may start to ask a second set of questions:

Could my life be this amazing all the time?

What is possible if I focus on what I want in life?
Should I share this approach with my friends and family?

These questions may not have direct answers either. However, your story will likely go one of two ways:

1. **The first set of questions wins.**

   When this happens, you retreat to the life you were living prior to poking your head out of your comfortable cocoon. These questions stem from fear of perception, low self-trust, insecurity, and playing small. They are low-energy questions, and they cause you to shrink backward into the rut you have lived for so long.

2. **The second set of questions wins.**

   When these questions win, you continue to be curious, to notice, and to sit with questions that do not necessarily have concrete answers. These questions stem from honesty, self-acceptance, empowerment, and authenticity. They are higher-energy questions, and they cause you to stretch toward a bigger, brighter version of yourself.[42] The rut is still there for you to revisit, but the new paths are so beautiful and abundant that the old rut is not nearly as appealing as it once was.

Neither approach is right or wrong. I spent a decade vacillating between both sets of questions before fully leaning into option two. For me, the first set of questions limited my freedom, peace, and abundance. It was as if I was half-in, half-out of living the life I craved. I was on a repeat loop, pretending everything was okay while wrestling with the ongoing tension of discontent. The bubbling from within continued. It caused me to keep playing with the idea of surrender. Especially when moving in and out of jobs or relationships, I noticed that I fretted about what others would think. I sought input to influence my decisions. I was reliant on others.

To get to the calm, one must persevere beyond the first set of insecure questions to reach the second, growth-oriented set of questions. When I finally arrived at these, I was so ready that there was no stopping me. I became laser-focused on my intentions: freedom, trust, love, and abundance. There were three clear actions I practiced to be in relationship with my intention.

First, I practiced the pause. The pause allows me to gauge my interest in relationships and commitments. It enables me to reground in my intentions multiple times throughout a day. The four-step process I use is a variation of a lesson offered through Cognitive Behavioral Therapy.[43] My process is:

1. **Stop.**
   Literally, stop. Push the pause button. Life is hectic. Stopping, even for a moment, is a profound act of power. Stopping allows us to be present.

2. **Listen (Connect).**
   The instruction of listen reminds me to go within and connect with myself. I get to check-in with my own feelings and thoughts. This moment of listening and connecting causes me to be human by paying attention to myself and others.

3. **Choose.**
   Responding and reacting are easy defaults for me. Realizing that I have an active role in choosing my path multiple times per day creates a radical reawakening within me. Choosing allows me to be engaged and responsible for myself.

4. **Act.**
   Action creates forward movement.

This process enables me to quickly refocus on my intentions. It is important to note that all four steps are required for maximum impact. I have noticed when I cut corners and only Stop and Act I miss the richness of Listening and Choosing. Or if I Stop, Listen, and Choose but never Act, I create an incomplete cycle for myself. I fall short of creating my intention.

Cultivating curiosity was the second action to bring me into relationship with my intention. This comes in the form of open-ended questions to myself and others. The lens of curiosity allows me to lay down the burden of acting like I have it all figured out and buttoned up. I do not have to be on the same life path as everyone or anyone else to create success and fulfillment in my life. Shifting language and coming from curiosity supported my journey to calm.

Finally, I shared my plans with others. This was not to seek their input, rather to continue moving toward my intention. I built a team of cheerleaders. I told them what I was up to, invited their support, and got busy living the life that truly fueled me.

With these three steps, the chatter in my head quieted and I became focused. I trusted my process of discovering the next step, every step of the journey. I worked through the mechanics of reprioritizing my time and commitments. A calm presence filled me.

Midlife calm is engaging your whole self. It is greater than a prescribed message of who you should be, what you should do, how you should think and feel, or how fast you should act. Midlife calm is honoring the parts of you that have been dormant and inviting them to come out and play. It is releasing the limitations placed on you, whether by others, society, or yourself. It is releasing your arms so you can work with both hands, instead of labeling one hand dominant and deeming the other restricted. It is becoming whole and proceeding from that place.

Midlife calm is embracing a "both and" way of life. This is when you are *both* in contribution to others *and* committed to your own care and growth. It is playing big, embracing possibility, and being open to delight.

Midlife calm is being intentional and making powerful choices that align with who you are and what you are up to. It is being clear about the bigger Yes in life and being committed even through the pull of peer pressure, tiredness, temptation, and triggers. Midlife calm is honoring what has occurred and stopping there, without entanglement in stories and past pains. It is coming to the place where the past simply is. Midlife calm is knowing the present and future are ripe with new opportunities. It is being curious about yourself. Midlife calm is stretching beyond your comfort zone, which can be fun, freeing, and feel good.

Midlife calm is the culmination of our choices. Some choices lead you down a path that is not fully aligned with who you are. These are not necessarily poor choices. Typically, you do the best you can with the information available. There is a cultural pressure to pursue success, and choices are often tainted by that pressure. Midlife calm is embracing that life is happening for you, not to you.

When years of choices have pulled you out of alignment, at some point, your body and mind force you to a screeching halt. It is as if something inside yells, *"Whoa, Nelly! You do not get to go any further. You did not self-adjust, so now calibration is being forced upon you."* The moment you start to listen, embrace a new, empowering set of questions, and begin the work of realigning with your truth, you invite calm.

With that, it is time for a new Wikipedia entry:

Midlife Calm is a complete unveiling of identity and self-confidence that can occur in individuals, age 16 to 106. The phenomenon is described as the melting away of societal expectations to the point that the individual can hear their own true inner voice. It is a shift from thinking and doing to being one's authentic self. It occurs when a person merges the wisdom of societal norms and their own self-knowledge to create a unique path suited to their happiness. This may produce feelings of freedom, abundance, elation, joy, and/or the desire to fulfill one's life's calling.

Calm may be experienced in countless ways by countless individuals. For me, it could be plopping down on the couch with a contented sigh after a day of connection. Calm can also look like radiant energy, pouring forth in the form of laughter, conversation, and connection. At times, calm most certainly looks like dancing with abandon, whether alone or with others.

The dictionary defines calm as "free from agitation, excitement, or disturbance." My definition of calm is "acceptance and embracing." When I accept and embrace my thoughts, my body, my experiences, my desires, and my commitments, I do not get wrapped up in judgement, righteousness, or expectations. I am calm. And when I am calm, the world is my oyster!

During my journey toward calm, I experienced a powerful awareness. Before that, however, I got catfished.

I had returned to the dating world after my divorce. Although it was a bit rocky at first, I gradually found my sea legs in the dance of dating as an adult. Or so I thought. I corresponded with a man I found interesting and engaging for four and a half months. As soon as arrangements were made to meet in person, he disappeared. Fortunately, it was not in a primetime television-worthy catfishing experience. I did not empty my bank account or otherwise relinquish my life.

Dating as an adult has offered countless lessons and even more entertaining stories. Despite knowing myself more authentically than ever before and genuinely craving an intimate connection, I would often fall back into old ways. On dates, I would catch myself being extra accommodating, giggling at lame jokes, and too easily picking up the tab.

One friend observed that I became like a damsel in distress when dating. I hated that feedback, but she was right. Something about the dating dynamic brought me back to being an immature little girl, seeking acceptance and approval. And adult men come with their own baggage. Past betrayals, general hurt, and conflicted masculinity do not often make for a winning combination.

For eight years I toggled between being all in and all out. I would manage multiple dating profiles, then jump back to focusing solely on professional advancement and maintaining the status quo in my personal life. Name an app and I probably tried it. While I met some good guys along the way, I mostly met men who were unavailable, jaded, inauthentic, disconnected, or only pretending to be ready or interested.

I also met myself. I gradually discovered a truth that I was not initially prepared to accept. While I was meeting those men, it was me who was unavailable, jaded, inauthentic, disconnected, and only pretending to be ready or interested.

For any man or woman reading this, please take this to heart: It does not require eight years to get clear with yourself! Despite being a good student and quick learner, I unwittingly chose the uphill trek for my path of adult dating. You can be clear in far less time than I did. Actually, stepping into your midlife calm can enable this very result.

The long, arduous terrain of dating I embarked upon was my own decision. I actively made the choice to be okay, show up with a smile, and keep trying. I was playing a part I thought was necessary to connect with a man. Yet without the willingness to get honest with myself, I felt disappointed and dejected over and over. I was going through the motions and doing the right stuff without being my genuine self.

So, after another disappointment in love came in that moment when I was ghosted, I chose to get away and care for my soul. I went to Detroit, a place I deeply love. Bundled up on a cool morning, I walked to a place with a majestic view of Canada and started people watching. I was in a bit of a daze, just being still, occasionally creating a story in my mind about the people passing by.

A stroller approached. Somehow, I became fully alert and engaged. That baby looked at me with big, wide eyes, and held my gaze. It struck me that as adults, we do not often hold eye contact with one another. I suddenly felt really seen. I almost instinctively and sheepishly broke eye contact, as though we were creating a moment too raw or intimate for such a causal acquaintance.

Then, I started to think: is this what's going on? Are we not being seen anymore? Have we accumulated masks to fit in, go with the flow, and excel? Have we reduced one another to cogs, either helping or hindering our process of acquiring and achieving everything we want?

When a child innocently looks at us, we are deeply seen. If you can slow yourself enough and hold another's gaze without judgement, a moment of calm can be created, no matter how fleeting or unusual. We can gain something from one another, an interconnectedness from being deeply seen, if we only allow it.

I never broke eye contact with that child. His head turned to hold my gaze as his mom pushed the stroller forward, and then he was gone. Tears welled in my eyes. I was filled with a feeling of peace. He played a huge part in healing me in that moment. Thanks, kiddo. May you always be wide eyed and willing to connect.

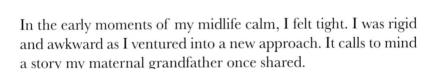

In the early moments of my midlife calm, I felt tight. I was rigid and awkward as I ventured into a new approach. It calls to mind a story my maternal grandfather once shared.

There was a little boy who came into the general store. A jar of candy sat on the counter next to the register for people to enjoy. Seeing the candy, the little boy's eyes grew as big as silver dollars.

His hand dove straight into the jar. He wrapped has fingers around as many pieces as his little fist could hold. When he went to pull his handful of loot out, he realized his fist was too big to pass through the mouth of the jar. He had everything he wanted in that fistful of candy, however, he could not have it. So close, yet so far.

There are two morals to this story. The first is that there are many solutions available to most situations. The little boy could have used his thumb and pointer finger to pick several pieces of candy out of the jar, one by one. He could have tipped the jar over and dumped several pieces out. He could have used the scoop sitting on the counter. He did not see all the possibilities available, so he did not get what he wanted.

The second moral of the story is that we do not have to hold onto things so tightly to have them in our lives.

To enter my midlife calm, I had to acknowledge how tightly I was holding onto the notion of making a certain amount of money and holding a specific title. I had to pay attention and make space to listen to my desires. As it turns out, I had every one of those desires immediately available if only I relaxed my grip and trusted myself. I have freedom, creativity, wealth, and even my desired title. I am the CEO of my life, and now my business.

The beauty of the calm is that it is always there. It is always available. All that was required to arrive at my midlife calm was getting out of my own way.

The next phase of my process felt like a swinging pendulum. Some moments I felt clear and confident in the decisions I was making to create a life I loved. Other moments felt as if I was tethered to other's expectations, which kept me from soaring. During this transition period, I happened upon a YouTube video that offered some perspective to my oscillation. In this video, famous author, speaker, and coach Tony Robbins speaks of the six needs of every human.[44] The first four are fundamental needs: certainty, uncertainty, significance, connection. The last two offer fulfillment: growth and contribution beyond self. The delineation of these six needs of every human supported me in the midst of stepping into my midlife calm.

If you are like me, you crave the certainty of schedules, specific roles, and established relationships. Like many, the instant I secure structure and certainly in any of these realms, I get bored. That is because I also need uncertainty. Robbins explains this as the need for variety, surprise, adventure, and excitement.

In a similar way, every decade of my life has entailed a different quest for significance. First at school, then at work. Western culture promotes standing out, being unique, and being special. It fuels us. Yet, as soon as I stand too far apart in my uniqueness, I revert to seeking connection and love. Again, the vacillation between two extremes.

If you are intentional, you stretch into growth and contribution, both of which offer fulfillment. Stepping out of your comfort zone is a familiar conversation. Yet what is often missing is identifying what zone, exactly, you step into. As many wise souls before me have, I propose that when you venture out of your comfort zone, you step into your growth zone. By giving it a name, you quickly acclimate to the energy and excitement that accompanies growth.

Unfamiliar experiences do not automatically equate to uncomfortable experiences. Consider babies and teens experiencing growth spurts. Although these refer mainly to physical growth, they are good reminders that we do not always get to choose if or when we grow. Sometimes growth is thrust upon us. Whether teething, shooting up in height by a couple inches, or being overwhelmed by the sudden flood of reproductive hormones, growth is something we have all experienced from day one of living.

We also have experience resisting growth. Have you ever spun a story of being fine with where you are, not wanting to stretch beyond what you know, or simply wanting things to remain the same? The undeniable truth, however, is that fulfillment in life is a result of growth.

Fulfillment also results from contributing beyond oneself in a significant way. This can be accomplished at any age. With the support of his parents, my seven-year-old nephew decided to raise money for the local Ronald McDonald House. He dutifully went to the store to gather items from the organization's wish list. It made him feel so good that he has made this an annual birthday tradition.

Nathan also brings others into the experience by inviting family and friends to contribute to the charity instead of splurging on him. It has become a triple win for Nathan, his tribe, and the residents of the Ronald McDonald House. To be clear, in addition to supporting his charity of choice, I also buy Nathan a birthday gift! No one goes without. This is often the case when we choose to be in contribution. Whether you help a neighbor carry groceries, raise funds for a worthy cause, or call someone who is lonely, contributing beyond yourself is powerful business.

Getting familiar with Robbins' six human needs helped me understand the swinging pendulum was part of the process of shifting into my midlife calm. When I draw my attention to these six categories, I easily see what is missing and where I am overcompensating. They simultaneously offer simplicity and depth. I was actively finding my center point. I was getting crystal clear about who I was and how my every day actions supported the authentic version of myself.

Can you recall a time when you were crystal clear? When every part of you aligned to focus in one direction? When you were able to silence the external noise of life to a point that you could stop, listen, choose, and act as opposed to reacting, responding, and retaliating?

My senior year at Xavier University started off typical. I was finally getting the hang of balancing school, an internship, and social life. I could coast through a few easy classes after front-loading my requirements as an underclass woman. My post-graduation plans were solidifying.

Those plans mostly revolved around the Jesuit Volunteer Corps. Their program entailed a year-long commitment to four core principles: community, simplicity, spirituality, and service. My first pick for placement was Anchorage, Alaska, and I was to report for duty in August. One of the program's requirements was a clean bill of health. When I went to see my doctor, we discovered a lump in my neck.

My life immediately went into turbo mode. I drove from the top to bottom of Ohio for appointments with various doctors. I underwent a full surgical thyroidectomy to obliterate a cancerous lump. Meanwhile, I struggled to complete my senior year of college and an internship. Finals. Packing. Graduation.

Then, a rigorous, month-long fast to starve my body of iodine. This was followed by a radioactive iodine treatment, follow-up appointments, and finally – thank God – recovery. I packed for Alaska, went on a long-awaited family cruise, and prepared for my sister's wedding. It was all so much.

Yet, the whole time, I was crystal clear. I was moving to Alaska to provide a year of service. Nothing could stop me. Not even cancer.

The external noise was loud, and the internal noise was hectic.

As soon as the word cancer was uttered, my fear was immediate and debilitating. Ultimately, the noise did not matter. Calm – or relative calm, at least – won.

Silencing the external (and some internal) noise in order to access my inner voice was the way through what otherwise may have been a story of an early life crisis. Without being able to name the strategy at the time, I steadied the pendulum swing by building what was seemingly missing. Uncertainty was thrust into my life, so I embraced certainty by staying the course of my plan. Significance appeared, causing me to stand out from my peers as I was handed a cancer diagnosis. So, connection was called into action – through family, friends, medical professionals, and a broad community of prayer support. Creating this balance caused the external noise to quiet. In the quiet, I could hear my inner truth guiding me to accept support, trust the process, and hang on to my intention of serving in Alaska. Every moment was comprised of the stop, listen, choose, act practice and a radically committed support system.

I laid around my parent's house that summer, completely depleted of hormones and nutrients my body craved. But we got through the summer. We had an impromptu wedding shower on the cruise for my sister. I got to do her hair and stand by her side as she married her love. And I ultimately went to Alaska for my year of service.

Calm won. To this day, every time I choose calm, it wins. Choosing calm entails quieting the external noise, calibrating the swinging pendulum of thoughts and emotions, and listening to your inner voice.

This can be your truth too.

When I was young, I was enthralled by the yin and yang symbol. I would also geek out about the masks that represent the theater, especially when it was depicted by two masks – one sad and one happy. The dichotomies drew me in. As an adult, I continue to be attracted to the beauty and wisdom of contrasts.

> Without the agitation of sand,
>   an oyster does not produce a pearl.

> Without undergoing pressure,
>   coal does not become a diamond.

> Without breaking through the dark and heavy earth,
>   a seed does not grow above ground.

The yin and yang in Chinese philosophy suggest that opposite forces are in fact interdependent, interconnected, and complementary.[45] Yin is receptive, and yang is active. In coexistence they create balance, harmony, and wholeness.

I do not mean to suggest that without a crisis there would be no calm. Simply notice that agitation and pressure are not necessarily negative. They simply are. They are part of the whole. They produce strength and balance.

Calling agitation and pressure crises invites you to halt, resist, and retreat. Instead, what if you viewed moments previously deemed a crisis as opportunities that make your life whole and well-rounded? What if you invited the interconnected that exists between crisis and calm into your life? What if you accepted that one does not exist without the other, and therefore it is all welcome?

Calm is a way of being. It is a reality sourced from within. It allows us to show up to any situation present and powerful. It is proactive and intentional.

Rhythm is everywhere and humans rely on those rhythms. We are rhythmic beings. This shows up in the cycle of light and darkness through the day and year, as well as the seasons within each year. Your body depends on the rhythm of your breath which draws oxygen in and pushes carbon dioxide out. In a similar way, your heartbeat pumps blood throughout your body with a steady, consistent pace. Women's bodies typically follow a pattern of the menstruation cycle through childbearing years. And ocean tides are caused by the gravitational forces and the rotation of the earth.

Rhythm can be a powerful mechanism to stimulate engagement. Think about the last time a tune came on and without any thought, your foot started tapping, your hands started clapping, or you started singing. Rhythm is deeply a part of us.

When we notice and honor the rhythms in and around us, we can begin to embrace them. When we embrace, we lean into the beauty of cadence, both in moments of growth and life, and moments of rest and death. Trees are not bad for letting their leaves fall. Nor are they singularly beautiful in the spring.

Autumn is the season when things slow, dwindle, and shift into dormancy. Dormancy enables rest. Many are innately attracted to it for this reason. Autumn speaks to the genius of transition and slowing from one phase to another. Winter speaks to the gift of turning inward, being still, and preparing for rebirth. Spring speaks to the genius of birth and growth. Summer speaks to the gift of carefree play and adventure. The seasons offer wisdom and beauty that engage all our senses. They know the gifts of life and death, play and rest.

If I were to equate midlife calm with a season, it would be spring. Midlife calm is when we are in full bloom, stepping into a new life and way of being. It is what comes after you have done the work of incubation, receiving the lessons and nourishment that align you for growth.

You are a rhythmic being too. When you experience loss and death, you get to embrace life fully. Rest and death provide a pause for you to realign with your own unique beat. Pausing the noise around you to tune into your innate rhythms results in calm. Calm takes many forms, yet in each it represents the ultimate act of acceptance.

Rhythm is found by experiencing the ebb and flow of energy, growth, rest, and being. Being in constant motion, doing, energy, and growth risks a forced pause. This can look like sickness, apathy, lack, or chaos. Each offers its own lesson, but one of the greatest lessons is to simply embrace the rhythms of your unique life.

All of this comes full circle to the original questions: *"What does a midlife crisis mean to you?"* and *"What are some specific examples?"* It's like Paul Harvey used to say with dramatic inflection, "Now, for the *rest* of the story."[46] Below are some additional responses that provide a slightly different perspective.

A midlife crisis is a time where we start to assess our trajectory in life. We take a look at our current beliefs, views, perspectives, achievements and dreams and decide if this is where we want to continue heading or make changes toward a new vision.

Midlife crisis is a phase people often refer to when transitioning from not knowing who they are to knowing who they are. It is a beautiful moment: discovering what matters most in life, transitioning from being self-absorbed to world-focused, and looking for meaning in one's life. This transition can be initiated by many things. It feels like a midlife crisis when poorly experienced. It can also be a wonderful awakening to one's true gift for humanity. It can be the beginning of a focused life of contribution.

When the identity we put on meets who we really are. When one is tired of being suppressed, which is why so many drastic changes occur. It's a battle of identity that happens multiple times to some, or none for others. It depends on if we truly allow ourselves to live, or if we constantly invite and create rebirth in self.

…around fifty or so, you start to look at your life and wonder, 'What am I doing that serves others and feeds my soul?' This age aligns with kids leaving the nest, knowing you can have more freedom in your life, and can focus on fulfilling your own needs.

I always said that my midlife crisis was going to be really great. I wanted to travel the world and do something fun. It would be a time to take a break and do something for myself. Then I realized that life is now. Why not create that now? I started creating adventures and fun with my family. Every day there's the possibility that the end is now, so why not live life and experience it to the fullest? I've had so many obstacles in my life, but I continue to step over the boulders and climb the mountain. I see crisis as opportunity, like when I lost my job. This doesn't mean that I don't get emotional and have hard days, but the big so-called crisis doesn't resonate with me. I love aging! I'm blessed to live every additional day!

A crisis implies catastrophe or disaster. It's not often a crisis! It is usually uncharted territory or an unexpected dynamic, both of which can lead to new opportunities, options, and adventures.

Midlife crisis means that the unraveling has begun. We begin to seek answers inside ourselves, rather than outside of ourselves. We begin to question our belief systems and really start to look at why we act, react, or do things in a certain way, and evaluate whether it's serving us. We begin to search for our mission in life: why are we here, how can we serve, what is the purpose of our lives? It also leads to a shift in our way of being. We begin to focus outward, on how we can make contributions to the world. To me, the word crisis is misleading. It's truly an inward journey of self-discovery, shifts, and a deepening of self-love that allows for turning outward in love, and contribution to the world!

Do any of these sentiments align with your thoughts about midlife crisis? These responses certainly evoked a different feeling for me. These perspectives are forgiving and open to possibility. What possibilities are opening for you? What would it take to listen to your inner voice and trust that as much as you trust the expectations of external noise?

seven

With a deeper understanding of what midlife calm is, the next layer to explore is how to create if for yourself. I have begun layering examples to prime the pump. This chapter is specifically chock-full of perspective, considerations, and strategies that will lead you to your midlife calm.

I will begin with a question.

When was the last time you took a trip? I am willing to bet one of the first decisions was where you were going. Did you also get clear on what you wanted to experience? Or did you say you were going on a trip and that was it? You packed a bag – some cozy clothes in case you arrived on a mountain and a bathing suit in case you landed on a beach; and headed to the airport? No. That is not how it works. You had an intention to seek the sun or the silence of the country. You became clear on your intention (relaxed time, connection with family/friends, enjoying new cuisine, etc.) and the mechanics (buying the tickets, filling the car with gas, packing your bag, etc.) flowed from that space.

There is a powerful equation that represents this scenario and can be applied to every aspect of life. I was introduced to this through a transformational leadership program called Boston Breakthrough Academy.[47]

The equation looks like this:

$$Intention + Mechanics = Results$$

Allow me to share a few illustrations of how this equation plays out.

In 2019 I went on an adventure of a lifetime with my mom and dad. My dad coauthored *Peace Be With You*, a book and anti-bullying training manual for educators. He and his colleagues were invited to present at the World Anti-Bullying Conference in Dublin, Ireland. My paternal grandfather was a first-generation immigrant from County Waterford, but my dad had never traveled to his homeland.

Now, my mom has never had any desire to travel outside of the United States except for return visits to the Canadian side of Niagara Falls and a summer service program with my sister in Guatemala. So, I was tickled when she was clear and direct with her intention, *"I am going with you!"* I immediately followed, *"… and I am too!"* Our two-fold intention was clear: support dad and his colleagues as educators impacting the world; and create a once in a lifetime adventure. We knew when dad had to be in Dublin, and we also knew which days we would be free to explore the beauty of the countryside. From there, the mechanics were easy. I lined up flights, car rental, and lodging.

The trip played out as trips often do. I was cranky in many moments, my energy depleted from white knuckled navigation of the countryside. Yet, I wanted so badly to soak up every moment of this vacation. Dad was in physical pain from a sciatic nerve pinch, compounded by being squished in the back seat of the car. He was also battling some anxiousness about the conference and feeling out of his usual role of being the leader as he literally sat in the back seat throughout the journey. Mom was all energy, all the time, ready to seize the moment! She was aware and cared about the space both dad and I were in, however, she did not allow either of us to defuse her joy and wonderment.

All of this to say, the trip had some high tension and low energy moments. Still, it was truly a once in a lifetime adventure! From the moment the conference accepted dad's proposal, we were crystal clear on our intention to create a once in a lifetime adventure. The mechanics – when we arrived and left, driving from one night's stay to the next, and scheduled tours – were a small part of the equation. The big part was the intention. Because we remained grounded in the intention, our desired result was created.

When you recognize and treat your intention as a larger part of the equation than the mechanics, you shift from human doing to human being. This shift supports midlife calm. Another brilliant dynamic of this equation is that your results always point back to your intention. So, the equation looks like:

Intention + Mechanics = Results

Could mom, dad, and I have gotten caught up in the hiccups and hurdles of the trip? Yes. Could this have shifted into a memory of miserable moments? Yes. However, because we regrounded ourselves individually and as a team in our intentions, we created exactly what we wanted. The mechanics supported our intention. The results of our trip reflected the original intention to create a once in a lifetime adventure.

I am happy to share, some other parts of this adventure of a lifetime included an unexpected boat excursion to whale watch, dining on potatoes and brews in little pubs, a private tour of the Dublin Zoo, sleeping in a castle or two, finding neighborhood parks, celebrating the gifts dad brought to those he encountered at the conference, watching wild horses run the beach, drinking tea in the mornings as we looked out onto the water, hearing the Gaelic version of prayers in a shared Mass, and the rainbow that spanned across the sky the exact moment it needed to be there for all three of us.

Intention is powerful. Intention is a tool for the tactical and tangible moments of life, as well as for our internal space. It can center us in who we are and what we are up to. The example of going on a trip highlights the equation. This next story offers a different lens of the notion that Intention + Mechanics = Results. Following this example, I will show how this plays a role in midlife calm.

From an early age, one of my intentions was to serve seniors. I had a deep, innate love for older people and saw this population was underserved in many ways. This intention and love fueled my clarity to become a social worker in the field of geriatrics. I am fortunate. Many young people are not clear how their interests, gifts, and skills can create their vocation. Because I was clear, the mechanics associated with my intention flowed. I secured an undergraduate degree, gained professional experience, pursued a master's degree, and landed a job that would allow me to fulfill my intention of being a geriatric care social worker early in my career.

Consider for a moment, however, a young person who is not clear about what is meaningful and important to them. That young person is routinely asked, *"What do you want to do when you grow up?"* This question focuses on doing instead of being. It pushes the young person to focus on a day in the future when what they do professionally becomes enmeshed with who they are. The question is about a role, a responsibility, a hat they will wear as opposed to being curious about who they are in the moment and how that can be accentuated in all the roles, responsibilities, and hats they will ultimately wear throughout life. The question we ask young adults places emphasis on the mechanics and thus skews the power of the equation.

To be clear, the question of *"what do you want to do when you grow up?"* is comfortable because it is focused on external, tangible, measurable outcomes. The opportunity is to be open to asking a new question. And the opportunity is to recognize that asking a different question is not uncomfortable so much as it is unfamiliar. Shifting the question from *"What do you want to DO?"* to *"Who ARE you and who do you want to BE?"* opens a dialogue that acknowledges the whole person. It places the emphasis on being grounded in intention before getting clear on the mechanics.

Other cultures embrace that humans are beings more than doings. The Japanese language has the word *ikigai*, which means "life purpose."[48] *Ikigai* is what causes a person to jump out of bed in the morning and keep going all day! It is the source of joy that each individual is intimately aware of for themselves. In fact, there is no word equivalent in the Japanese language to 'retirement.'[49] *Ikigai* is a broader, overarching intention of life that reaches before, throughout, and after working years. It serves as the source – the intention – for how the person pursues relationships, work, and hobbies.

Let that sink in. What if, from the moment we were born, we asked, *"What is your life's purpose?"* Could such intention and focus allow our relationships and career to flow from that clarity? It is a very different question than, *"What do you want to be when you grow up?"* or *"What do you do?"* These questions pale in comparison to the sharing and self-awareness that are created when asked, *"What's your life purpose?"* This question invites attention to the intention, the core of who a person is. It is like choosing a destination and then packing accordingly as opposed to vice versa.

The genius of midlife calm is being deeply connected with the intention of life. Your intention invites you to periodically step away from the tasks and commitments in order to gain a clear picture of what matters to you as an individual. Stepping off the hamster wheel, or checking out of the rat race, gives us the bandwidth to enter a space that is catered to who we are as individuals. In healthcare, this is called person-centered care.[50] In business, it is called customer-centric culture.[51] When you begin to focus on your mission, your gifts, and your purpose on earth in this moment and time, clarity and possibilities emerge. You step into the reality that your results always point back to your intention. Your results are a direct outcome of your intentions.

In the past, I wanted to be a CEO. Throughout my career, I was always subordinate to someone. I placed all my efforts and energy into mechanics: seeking jobs where I could move up the ladder, finding projects to demonstrate my abilities, and committing to everyone else's success. I was caught in doing. Little did I know, I had yet to sincerely set my intention to being a CEO. As soon as I shifted my intention the results aligned. Today, I am the CEO and Founder of Potere Coaching. The exciting part is that I did not have to know all the answers from the onset. When I invested and reinvested in my intention, the mechanics became manageable.

When I got grounded in my commitment to be a CEO, I realized my intention was to be a powerful, humble, authentic and courageous woman. Shifting my focus to practicing each of these attributes created momentum that caused me to step into the logistics of being a CEO with substantially more ease and flow. This means you get to be clear and intimate with your intention. Be curious. Go deep. Explore what lies beneath the intentions you have in your life. Who do you get to be to realize your intentions? Begin practicing those ways of being immediately. There is no right or wrong way. You get to find your own rhythm, which means you get to step into the dance of your life!

If you have any doubt around the power of intention, consider Viktor Frankl's survival of Nazi concentration camps. Frankl was forced to work in the freezing cold, with minimal nourishment, separated from his wife and children. In *Man's Search for Meaning*, he shows how optimism, purpose, and hope gave him an edge in surviving. He committed to the intention of being reunited with his wife and children. Despite never being reunited, the intention was the powerful source of life for him. It was an anchor and guiding light through literal hell.

Getting clear on your intentions is a necessary step in living your midlife calm. Being in relationship with intention is a practice. My invitation is to begin practicing now.

Set this book down and journal on the following questions.

Who are you?
Who do you want to be?
What is your life's purpose?
When you are at your best, what qualities do you notice within yourself?

Welcome back. I trust that the time of reflecting and journaling about who you are was a gift. I acknowledge you for investing time and attention in yourself. For some, this may have been a new endeavor. If it felt foreign, that is ok. Remember unfamiliar experiences do not automatically equate to uncomfortable experiences. Read that again. Let that land.

Shifting a portion of our time, attention, and energy from mechanics to intention may be an unfamiliar practice at first because you are stepping out of what you know. You are stepping out of your comfort zone. The image below offers a visual representation. Seeking safety, control, and comfort confines us to a small existence. This is our comfort zone. By staying within the comfortable container we create for ourselves, we miss out on acquiring new skills, conquering goals, finding our purpose, and living our dreams. These are our learning and growth zones. Yet, those opportunities are exactly what I crave! The plot twist, as shown in the illustration, is that in order to have those realities, I must push through what I will encounter upon stepping out of my comfort zone – fear, excuses, and lack of confidence. Only by stretching through the fear zone can I land in the space of learning and growth.

Comfort Zone

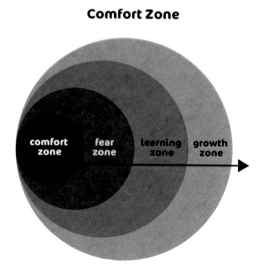

As you practice leaping out of your comfort zone, it is important to know that a portion of your brain is wired for survival and safety.[52] It tells you to stay in your comfort zone. When you start to move out of it, your amygdala causes adrenaline, cortisol and other hormones that trigger fight or flight signals to be released. As you dip your toe into the waters just beyond your comfort zone, your sympathetic nervous system engages. When you retract too quickly, you miss the reality that the waters of fear may not be as deep or cold as you thought. Learning, growth, and continual expansion are within reach. The tried-and-true way to break through fear is to be intentional. It allows you to rewire your brain to see that you can be safe outside your comfort zone. You can align with truth instead of the external noise.

Midlife crisis is often a label placed on a person pushing beyond their comfort zone. A question to ponder is, what is the crisis here? Are you simply feeling the movement from small to big, from shackle to freedom, from constriction to expansion? Are you stretching into new space that aligns with your intention? Is it simply unfamiliar?

To be clear, I still sink back into my comfort zone. I am human, after all. However, I live more predominantly in the learning and growth zones now. They fuel my calm, courage, authenticity, love, abundance, and more. It is a process, not a destination. The trick is to make sure the process is fun. If you have made it this far, you probably want to live life more than you want to settle for a numb, mediocre version of yourself. So, let's keep going!

Becoming aligned with your inner voice and truth is the next step of venturing into your midlife calm. This step blends the gifts of intention and language. I am willing to bet walking through an example of losing weight will resonate with some people reading this book. The intention is clear, yet often we immediately set ourselves up for failure with the language we use.

A couple summers ago, I registered myself in a twelve-week nutrition program at a local hospital. I have battled the bulge for years, using food as a friend in high and low moments. This step of participating in a nutrition program was an act of enlisting and receiving support. An act that was somewhat unfamiliar in the story I told about myself. I was independent and did not want to show weakness of flaws or inconsistent discipline and motivation. As we all know though, the definition of insanity is doing the same thing and expecting different results. So, I pursued a different approach. Every week for three months, I spent money, attended meetings, reviewed my intake with a registered dietician, and got on a scale in front of another human. At the time, I weighed two-hundred and forty pounds. My goal was to lose seventy pounds over the course of twelve months.

"I want to lose 70 pounds (or fill in whatever your number is)." Take a moment to notice the inaccurate language those of us who seek to lose weight have engrained in our vocabulary and therefore etched into our brains and our entire psyche. There are two immediate dilemmas with this statement. First, just because I want something does not mean I get it or even that I work for it. Wanting places your desires outside of you. Wanting casts a curtain of uncertainty and relinquishment of control as to whether that desire will be fulfilled. Wanting can trap you in mental wanderings that keep your desires perpetually out of reach.

The invitation is to powerfully declare all that is within your vision and intention for a fulfilled life. For over a decade, I have said, *"I am rich"* when I pick up the tab for friends. I started saying this in my 30s – a time when I carried debt and was living paycheck to paycheck. Instead of living in scarcity, I decided to exercise strategic generosity. I leaped over the language of "I *want* to be rich" and went directly to "I *am* rich". This created a massive shift within me. Since starting this practice, possibilities have begun to appear. I find that my bills are paid, and I routinely have extra resources to share. I also have others delight me by picking up the tab more often than I could ever imagine.

Wanting and declaring are two very different dynamics. Declaring requires you to be honest with yourself and willing to leap out of your comfort zone. What do you notice within yourself when you powerfully declare your desires? What possibilities present themselves when you get clear on your intention and declare it gets to happen?

Also, returning to the topic of losing weight, how often is losing something a positive experience in life? When I lose my car keys, I go into a frenzy. When I lose a loved one, I am saddened that I no longer get to be with them in human form. Most things I lose, I am eager to find. To be clear, I do not want to lose weight. I do not intend to find it again after I lose it! It is important to use the word *release* weight. Your language tells your brain what you are up to so it can fall in line and get to work on what you are declaring. If your language is weak, you will find every loophole to remain comfortable.

It is also important to be specific on the amount and by when. For me, it sounded like this: I am committed to releasing 70 pounds by September 2020.

To accomplish my goal, I enlisted support. For twelve weeks, I drove through rush hour traffic to stand on a scale outside of the comfort of my home, participate in a class, and review my nutrition log. There were many times I did not want to attend, I would have rather worked late, or was not interested in the topic of the week. Admittedly, I did skip one of the sessions. But overall, I was committed – even if begrudgingly.

Over the course of twelve weeks, I lived a full spectrum of experiences: nervousness, diligence, disappointment, incremental success, and impatience. The dietician gave me the same feedback every week: reduce portion size, hydrate, alter the times of day I ate, etc. It was laborious. Ninety days into creating new habits of health and ways of being, I had released a total of seventeen pounds. Not too shabby, and I had fifty-three more to go.

According to a *21/90 Rule in Progress* published by Booksy Press, it takes 21 days to create a habit and 90 days to create a permanent lifestyle change.[53] I was well on the way, so I took another significant step. I researched, met with, and hired a personal trainer. I started going to a gym twice a week for ten months. When we went into lockdown during the summer of 2020, I continued with virtual training sessions. I was on a roll. I was getting stronger, feeling my energy increase, and seeing my muscles tone.

During the first part of my health journey, the nutritionist was not telling me anything I did not already know. Nevertheless, I told myself I did not want to do what she recommended the first many weeks. I was being defiant, resistant, and angry. I was firmly planted in my comfort zone. Then, I slowly ventured out. I allowed myself to be receptive, open, honest, and even playful with the experience. It unlocked the results I was seeking, and more. The trainer was an unanticipated part of my intention of being healthy. I could not name that part of the intention in the autumn of 2019, yet by January 2020, I was deep into committed action. The mechanics of becoming strong revealed themselves at just the right moment in my health journey.

The point here is that had I never taken the first step and met with the nutritionist, I would have never had the courage to meet with a personal trainer. This is what stepping out of your comfort zone looks like. Incremental steps and aligned language bring you to a place where you delightfully no longer recognize yourself. A place where you live your intentions and declarations.

Had I stayed in my comfort zone, I would have continued pretending that my intention was to release weight. My language would have mimicked wanting to be thinner in some distant day. I would have remained so focused on feeling embarrassed and self-conscious that I would have actually been committed to being embarrassed and self-conscious. As I stepped feebly out of my comfort zone, I found that it was not nearly as terrifying as I had made it out to be. Although I was in new territory, I was never actually uncomfortable. I felt curious, excited, and stretchy. All were new experiences. And you know what? I liked it! It can be exhilarating – if we say so.

As you shift into midlife calm, you will find there are ample support systems available. Some are tools and tactics; others are experiences and practices.

In coaching there is a tool called The Wheel of Life, an idea originally put forth by Paul J. Meyer in the 1960s.[54] This is an awareness exercise in which you identify eight to twelve categories to represent your life. Each category is labeled in a wedge of a circle, like slices of a pizza. On a scale of one to 10, you rank the amount of time and energy invested in each area, with 10 being the most and one being the least. Starting at the center point, the wedge is shaded to represent the score given to each area. Any wedge scored 10 is fully colored in, whereas any wedge scored five is halfway colored in.

The Wheel of Life is an exercise of honesty. You do not rank based on the time, energy, and attention you *want* or **believe** you should invest in each category. It is a point in time perspective. Once filled in, the results clearly demonstrate whether your wheel would roll smoothly, or whether there would be massive divots that create bumps or even a complete stop in your life.

Of course, being human, your wheel of life will always flex and change. The goal is awareness, not perfection. Perhaps one of your wedges is spirituality, and you currently rank that as a one. Perhaps another area is rest (which is different than sleep) and that is also ranked as a one. Perhaps vocation is a ten. The exercise helps us notice where our energy is invested.

This tool supports the practice of noticing without judgement or comparison. It serves as a point in time benchmark that can be revisited and reassessed. It offers a visual representation of growth and personal alignment. The Wheel of Life allows you to honor that where you are right now is exactly where you are meant to be. It also invites you into curiosity as to where you want to grow from here. Clarity, possibility, and growth all exist when working from the whole.

The Wheel of Life is an external tool that can inform midlife calm. As you may have guessed, there are also internal tools that inform our journey into midlife calm. Stepping into the calm requires attention to what happens in our bodies, as these are clues available to guide us.

I once coached a client who described her experience in two distinct ways. *"I feel like the top of my head has opened up and a giant washing machine full of rainbow-colored foam bubbles are spouting out!"* And: *"It's like a white light surrounding me, spilling out and beyond my body. I feel safe, calm, love."*

In our early sessions, she had a tight chest, slumped shoulders, an upset stomach, and headaches. Gradually, together we shifted her to lightness, radiating energy, and a sense of peace. Her muscles were no longer tight. Her head stopped splitting. Her stomach could digest food without cramping.

Part of the early coaching experience was a process of getting in touch with what was happening within her body. The tightness and discomfort were clues that something was misaligned. I call these the rumble strips of life. They are a warning that you are too close to the edge and venturing any further out of personal alignment may be dangerous.

As always, you have a choice. You can continue to veer off and have an accident, or you can come back into alignment. Your body's indicators when you are at risk of danger may come in the form of an ache or pain, diminished senses, or a lack of energy and desire. You can choose to ignore these red flags, or you can align with your highest and best selves. Choosing alignment is choosing midlife calm.

This calls to mind the classic story of how to boil a frog. To be clear, this is simply to illuminate a message. I do not condone hurting frogs.

If a frog is dropped into a vat of boiling water, it will jump out to save itself. However, if it is placed in lukewarm water that is slowly brought to a boil, the frog will not perceive the danger and will be cooked to death.

If we are the frogs and life is the pot, is it possible that we are unwittingly falling victim to the heat of expectations, speed, and comparison? When our bodies cry out, it is an opportunity to jump out of the boiling water and find a place of peace.

For me it was a moment of acknowledging that working at the zoo was not the right fit for me. It was incredible in every way, yet not for me in that season of life. And that was okay.

This simple acknowledgement unlocked potential. It immediately produced a feeling of levity. I felt free, more at ease with my skills, more confident in my ability to show up. I told myself that I was not required to take any action in response to this acknowledgement. I simply let it be.

This opened me to possibility and ultimately flowed into my authentic vocation of coaching. Being in the space of acknowledgement gently softened my resistance. It unlocked the calm that had been available all along, cloistered away until I was prepared to embrace it.

The bottom line is that midlife calm is not a moment. It is the process of pulling back the curtains, becoming still, and getting attuned to who you are. It has been within you all along. You simply had to develop the interest, hunger, curiosity, trust, or whatever it was that drove you to be invested in your true self.

Throughout life, I would be annoyed and disconnect anytime I heard the cliché "trust the process." In the journey of my midlife calm, I have come to realize life is the process, and I am life. Therefore, "trust the process" means trust myself. Fortunately, midlife calm is a journey that cannot be unlearned, only consistently practiced and refined. The process is exponential and builds upon itself. As I trust myself, I am clear about my intention and I take action. As I act toward my intention, I trust myself and live in a place of midlife calm.

There are more clues and tools for you to leverage in the process of growing into your midlife calm. One of these is your inner voice, which is pure and honest. Your inner voice speaks from a clear vision of what is possible. It is not burdened by fear. When I have chosen to ignore my inner voice there were consequences. Those consequences, albeit painful and unfortunate at times, are all part of my story and have brought me to this moment. They have also helped solidify my commitment to midlife calm. Turning inward to listen and trust myself are the actions that continue to guide me to deeper calm and fulfillment.

Your inner voice serves as a compass if you allow it. Whether you mute it for a day, year, or decade, it is always willing to speak when you are ready to listen. As I run with my inner voice, most often I do not know all the answers. Yet I trust myself enough to be clear with my intention and follow through with committed action. This combination of self-trust and action have been vital to my midlife calm. Check in with your inner voice a moment:

What is your inner voice calling you to create in this moment of life?

What is bubbling up from within?

How can you stoke your inner fire to burn bright?

Where do you notice resistance?

Where do you notice excitement?

Your calm may be bubbling with energy. It may be still. It could be curious. It could be joy. It can be many things and experienced in many ways. Midlife calm represents nestling into who you are. Noticing yourself. Giving space for the inner wisdom.

As you continue practicing paying attention to your body, listening to your inner voice, and nestling further into who you are, the next available gift are your senses. Your five senses are also stellar north stars for claiming your midlife calm.

I notice that I can especially connect to my five senses when I go for a walk. Like many, I strive for ten-thousand steps per day. I spent one recent walk profoundly aware of my midlife calm. I felt in alignment with my relationship with myself. My posture was straight, shoulders held back, head tall, chin up. I noticed and connected with my breath, letting the air entirely fill my lungs before exhaling it all out.

During this walk, I stopped to pet three cats I came upon. They were soft and friendly. Two of the cats were skinny with protruding ribs. They probably survived on scraps and what they could hunt. The third was fluffy and beautiful. You could tell that it was well-fed and well-loved. Further down the block, I smelled the exhaust from a junker van as it took off. I passed a woman who appeared to be in her nineties, tending to her pristine front yard. Birds were singing in the trees. All of my senses were activated.

Suddenly, out of nowhere, I was jolted out of being present by a sequence of thoughts:

I need to get organized.
I have four hours left before I need to meet up with my friend.
I have to get a whole laundry list of things done.
I need to accomplish, accomplish, accomplish!

If not for my midlife calm, the whole day would have likely been hijacked. I would have readily snapped back into my comfort zone, fixated on things that felt like a burden and depleted my energy. Instead, I found myself in the space of transition: moving from being in the calm, snapping out of it, and very capably shifting back in. Being connected to my five senses allowed me to remain calm. This is a powerful tool. By tuning into your senses, you ground yourself in the present and reconnect. This is important in every season of life, and especially during transitions.

When I get present, I can momentarily release the frantic feeling and the pressures of my to-do list. Yes, the laundry still gets to be managed. The bills get to be paid. However, these activities become easily accomplished when approached from a place of less resistance and pressure.

What do you notice when you pause and connect with what you see, smell, hear, taste, and feel? How does your body respond to the crisp air? Do you prefer your eyes to gaze upon a scene or take in the details? What smells elicit peace, presence, and calm for you? What can you let go of for a moment to become present and connected just as you are?

The journey into midlife calm is available to you. Here. Now. Are you interested in aligning with your human beingness as much or more than your human doingness? What is your intention for yourself? For your life? Practice and play with these tools. They are gifts in the process of discovering the calm that is waiting for you.

eight

There are times midlife calm is not an intentional choice. It can be thrust upon you by tragedy in the form of loss, whether that's death, divorce, job loss, or something else. Of course, this type of calm is different than the one I willingly embarked upon. Nevertheless, these unforeseen circumstances offer an opportunity. These life moments can send you inward and slow you down, both of which support the experience of midlife calm.

It is common to want to seek safety, security, and comfort when you feel as if life is happening to you, not for you...when you feel like you do not have a choice. Consider a feral cat. When this cat is wandering the streets, although possibly scruffy, it is likely a survivor – strong, smart, and quick – all to ensure its independence and freedom. It often knows where to find or hunt food and how to duck into a bit of shelter when the weather insists.

Now, think about this cat getting caught in a cage. It will tend to do one of two things. It will either lash out and hiss at anything that comes near trying to protect itself. Or the caged cat might push its body into the smallest possible position in the corner of the cage. It retracts into a space where nothing can approach it. Humans behave in similar ways. We seek safety by getting small and retracting, or by lashing out to keep everyone at a distance.

There is a difference between a freely chosen midlife calm versus one thrust upon us. The questions we tend to ask ourselves have a different tone.

Why did this have to happen?
I'm not ready.
It's too soon.
I just wish I understood why.
How am I going to get through this?

These are questions we have all encountered in life. These questions and feelings get to be noticed, observed, and tended to. If you fail to do so, you will not heal and you will not recognize the calm that is available.

This recalls a powerful analogy used in The Grief Recovery Method.[55] Imagine while out running errands you accidentally slip, fall, and break your leg. Would you go get medical treatment, repair the break, do therapy, and regain full functionality of your leg? Or would you get up and proceed without treatment or therapy, as if nothing ever happened? In this scenario, at the very least you spend the rest of your life with a limp.

No one can argue that the first option is the one most people choose. But when your heart breaks, you may not be as clear about what needs to be done to heal it. So, we often take the second option, proceeding through life with a crippled heart. To an extent, we are resilient. Often we are quick to address physical ailments while brushing emotional ailments under the rug. This does not serve anyone.

You and I get to heal what has been hurt in the past and continue to care for ourselves as other hurt inevitably occurs. Without taking this step, calm may feel elusive. It is *not* elusive though. Through healing, you can re-write stories from the past by honoring the facts and releasing the emotional charge. You can re-write your stories to glean the lessons, gifts, and gold within every situation. You get to show up aligned with yourself, instead of cowering in the corner or lashing out at anyone who dares to come near. Healing is a process that empowers midlife calm.

Jess, a dear friend and client, shared the following:

> *Part of what brought about one of my greatest metamorphoses to date was the loss of some very important people in my life. These people had complex lives, often carried dark secrets, and were burdened by heavy things. Yet at the same time, they had a levity and offered encouragement to me that was second to none. When they died within months of each other, I lost a lot. I also gained a lot. I freed myself from many dramas and traumas, both my own and those belonging to other loved ones.*

Jess was young when these losses occurred. While it is much more common for the loss of a parent to occur in midlife, Jess was in her twenties. She got to face her own mortality and her place in the world, and it caused her perspective to shift earlier than most. As a result, she had a chance to reset her thoughts and beliefs, and it changed her perspective on her life path. Those changes have been positive. Jess's term for this is the "re-write." She explains:

> *The rewrites are an opportunity to change the way we remember someone who has passed away. It is a chance to extract what was mainly good, instructive, and constructive, and to transform the narrative by which you forever remember them by.*

> *Rewrites are the empowering interpretation, and a conscious picking and choosing of the stories we tell. It gives us an opportunity to heal old wounds that could not and would not be mended in the midst of living. They give us hope and strength, and they honor the dead in a way that even the deceased may not have imagined. The rewrites are a chance for us to live how we all actually wanted all along, with a feeling of peace,*

love, and compassion in our hearts. Rewrites are not just for the dead. Rewrites are most especially for the living.

The re-write concept is powerful. It opens a space of possibility and allows each of us to author the life we are living. It enables you to create the story you are telling. It invites healing and the empowering interpretation in order to create calm in the midst of what may otherwise be deemed as crisis.

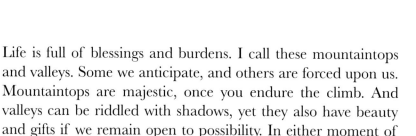

Life is full of blessings and burdens. I call these mountaintops and valleys. Some we anticipate, and others are forced upon us. Mountaintops are majestic, once you endure the climb. And valleys can be riddled with shadows, yet they also have beauty and gifts if we remain open to possibility. In either moment of life – mountaintop or valley – the tools of shifting into personal alignment support us in choosing the beauty, even when faced with a challenging scenario.

When I was a nineteen-year-old freshman at Xavier in Cincinnati, I met a man and fell in love. I will call him Matthew as I share part of our story. He was twenty-six and lived in Arkansas. We met in an AOL chat room. Yes, I am that person. We courted each other via long late-night calls and novel length emails in which we shared every part of ourselves with one another. I trusted him with every insecurity and secret, and he trusted me with the same. Matthew was gregarious and easily filled a room with his energy. I was enamored by an older, worldly man and the love he was pouring into me. Our connection was playful, connected, vulnerable and invested. As an international salesman, Matthew would tack on a trip to Cincinnati every couple of months so we could connect in person. I was committed to creating a life together. That was not the immediate plan, however. Matthew was afraid he was not the man I deserved, and fearful he would break my heart. And he did. Two years into sharing our lives, Matthew abruptly ended our relationship and married another woman two weeks later.

I did not see it coming. I was crushed. For months, my heart ached in a hollow, longing sort of way. My trust was severed, and my confidence plummeted. I felt abandoned and unwanted. I was deaf to my inner voice, to say nothing of the voices of those who knew and loved me. But this is only the first half of the story. The second half is even wilder.

Years later, after his marriage ended, Matthew and I reconnected. We rebuilt trust, dated, and got married. I was thirty. I loved his family and I loved him. My naïve mind thought our love could conquer all. In hindsight, I now understand that our relationship, although loving, was merely fulfilling Matthew's need to feel cared for and my need to be wanted. Matthew had significant physical ailments, which were complicated by addictions to alcohol and prescription narcotics. Our marriage devolved from being playful, connected, and invested to an infirmary where I was the perpetual nurse, and he was the patient. Neither of us were happy – individually or within our role as a couple.

On our third anniversary, we agreed that buying cards for one another would be trite. The marriage had been over for quite some time. As a practicing cradle Catholic, I never anticipated divorce being part of my life story. But after three years of balancing the roles of sole bread winner, caregiver, and pretending to also be a wife without any of the benefits of having a supportive partner, divorce was my idea. I needed it. I was numb and felt hollow, unsure of who I was. Despite my numbness, the pain of the divorce and the broken commitment was deep and raw. This pain took a huge amount of intentional effort and committed action to heal.

Two years later, I was driving to a Tuesday night baseball game in support of the Alzheimer's Association when I noticed a missed call from Matthew's aging parents. They were also deeply saddened by how things turned out, but they understood my decision. They continued to love me, while respecting the boundaries and loyalty to Matthew, their only and adopted child. There had not been a reason to call me in nearly two years.

The message on my phone was the kind, loving voice of Matthew's dad. *"Hi Krista. We're real sorry to bother you, but we were wondering if you could help us. We usually talk to Matthew every Sunday. We've been leaving him messages, but we've not heard from him and are starting to get worried. We hate to trouble you, but we don't know who else to call. Would you mind going over to Matthew's place and knocking on his door to check on him? Ask him to give us a call. We sure would appreciate it. So sorry to bother you. We sure do love you and thank you so much. Hope all is wonderful for you."*

I stayed at the game long enough to thank guests and donors and then, with a pit in my stomach, headed to Matthew's apartment. During our short marriage, I had arrived home to an unresponsive husband three times. I was accustomed to the fear of finding him dead. He always showed up with one more of his nine lives to spare though. Each time, I called 911, they administered Narcan in our home, then rushed Matthew to the hospital.

Upon arriving at his apartment that Tuesday night, I could hear the television inside. The lights were all on, and the door was unlocked. After several loud knocks, I popped my head into the apartment. A layer of dead gnats and flees covered the windowsill. Dirty dishes filled both sides of the sink and spread onto the countertop. Stacks of paper covered every inch of the kitchen table and cascaded onto the floor.

The noise and light heightened my senses. I had witnessed Matthew's hallucinations and aggression in the past. Both were caused by overuse of alcohol and prescription narcotics. Knowing that he owned guns, I yelled at the top of my lungs. *"Matthew! Matthew, are you here? Matthew, it's ok, it's me, Krista! Matthew, it's Krista. I'm coming in. Are you here? Matthew!"*

The next five minutes felt like hours. I methodically moved through the hoarded clutter with my back to the wall as I stepped into each new doorway. When I made it to the bathroom, I felt a swelling sickness when I realized I had to pull the shower curtain back to make sure he was not in the tub. I mustered the courage and yanked the curtain open. He wasn't there.

The spare bedroom was next. Its door was closed. I knew it was crammed to the brim with stuff, so I shifted my eyes to the couch. That was Matthew's usual spot. I felt sure I would find him there in a deep sleep. The sound of the noisy television mixed with the beating of my heart created a sensory overload within me. He wasn't on the couch, either.

Confusion overwhelmed me. My eyes darted to his bedroom. Nothing.

I turned off the TV. I needed to think. There was one last bedroom, but that too was a spare, cluttered with items behind a closed door. I was looking for clues but had no idea exactly what I was searching for. His bedroom was the last place to thoroughly check. I began moving toward his room when I stopped dead in my tracks, a few feet from the doorway.

Matthew was in bed asleep. The covers were pulled up around his shoulder. He was laying on his side, facing the doorway, with the lights on. I froze for several seconds. I had not seen him lying there when I looked in the room a moment ago. My brain could not process what was going on. I made two final attempts to loudly announce myself. I knew it would be startling to wake up to someone standing over you. With no response to those final yells, I felt my tone and urgency dwindle. I knew.

Still, my brain could not fully process what was going on. In what felt like a trance, I moved into the room and placed my hand on Matthew's forehead. I felt his neck for a pulse. Nothing. I was shocked. He looked comfortably asleep. I found his right hand and checked for a pulse on his wrist. Nothing. My first husband was dead.

I knew I needed to call the police, but I decided to take a moment to say goodbye. I sat at the foot of the bed. Jinx, Matthew's beloved, wildly mangy cat, suddenly burst into the bedroom. He had been outside for who knows how long and was hungry for love and attention. Together, Jinx and I sat in the valley with the body of the man we had loved.

The following weeks proceeded in turbo mode. My best friend helped me get Matthew's nineteen-year-old son to town within forty-eight hours. We removed dumpsters worth of clutter from the apartment. We coordinated with the coroner and Matthew's parents.

I was forced into the valley of shadow and doubt. Usually, I can focus and move through the mechanics of life even when my heart and mind are not fully invested. This was different. My parents and friends held me up. Coworkers picked up slack in ways I could not fully comprehend. It took several months to identify and honor the trauma I had lived through.

The entire experience caused me to turn inward and slow down. It was as if midlife calm had been thrown on me, like it or not. I certainly never wished for Matthew to die. He was only forty-two. But even in all the chaos, I found a blessing in knowing he was no longer experiencing chronic pain, loneliness, or isolation. This was the first beauty I identified in the valley. The second silver lining to this tragic story was the support I received from so many. These people have always been ready and willing to support me, but this moment caused me to surrender and be supported in a deep way. Asking for and receiving support has been one the greatest lessons and practices of my midlife calm.

The gifts continued. Matthew's parents and son were eager to rekindle our relationship. Today I am the godmother to the granddaughter Matthew did not live to meet. This spunky, wide-eyed child laughs freely and speaks her mind. His son and I have remained close through the decline and deaths of Matthew's parents. We found the beauty in what could easily be deemed crisis. We choose to rewrite the story and heal our hearts of the burdens that endured while Matthew was alive. Those moments were lived, and they get to be released so they are not perpetually lived. We chose to experience the beauty within the valleys and continue to climb to the mountaintops of life so we can share those beauties as well.

I did not choose this specific experience. Yet, through the pain and suffering, it opened my heart to others who are suffering. It gifted me with the ability to hold space for others experiencing grief and loss. It reinstated a relationship with Matthew's son. It is in these moments the idea that life is happening for us, not to us lands deep within my heart. Lessons abound, gifts are fruitful even in the valley of shadow and doubt – when we say so.

My invitation to you is to take a deep breath. I acknowledge that was a heavy story. I am certain you have your own as well. Continue to breathe into the possibility that there are lessons available within what has once – or always – been deemed a crisis. What if we used the tool of language and made a shift like

Thomas Edison did when he deemed every failure was actually a lesson? What if we shifted from crisis to calm?

There is more to explore as we seek additional clarity regarding midlife calm that feels forced upon us. I would like to unpack the cliché midlife crisis of a person having an affair. Although this is not something I condone, the example offers a perspective not often considered.

If I choose to have an affair, my partner may feel like our relationship was a fraud. He will probably feel hurt by my transgression. He will likely lack trust going forward. And, he will be angry, among many other thoughts and feelings. In confusion and bewilderment, our friends and family may look at the situation and determine that I am having a midlife crisis.

But upon digging deeper, it could be that I am listening to my inner voice. Perhaps I had doubts on my wedding day but proceeded to get married anyway. Now, years into my marriage, I make another choice. I connect emotionally, intellectually, and physically with someone else. I am seen and heard in a way that I have never been by my husband. I am more myself than ever before. Yet I have broken a commitment and hurt another.

What if instead of having an affair, the story went like this:

I have a vulnerable conversation with my husband. We listen to one another and explore possibilities. Through time and honest conversation, we determine that I am not living my best life.

He recognizes that he also deserves a partner who is invested in him. Together, we decide to end our marriage. I am free to live honestly. Eventually, I pursue another relationship.

Affairs happen for many reasons. Sometimes self-centeredness and lack of commitment are the culprits. Sometimes two people grow apart as a result of not mutually choosing to grow together.

But affairs can also happen when we get clear and calm about what we are up to in life. Clarity is created when we take time to notice ourselves and listen to our inner voice. This is different than going with the flow or accepting real or perceived external influences as the guiding force in one's life. The truth is, when I am not my best, it is likely my partner is not his/her best either. By engaging in an honest conversation and arriving at the decision and shared intention to work it out or to part ways, both people in the relationship are invited to live their best lives.

The scenario of engaging in an honest conversation creates space to be aware of our own wounds and confusion so we do not slip into a cascade of hurtful decisions and actions. Breaking a commitment, although it may seem like the necessary solution, is often not the best way to realize personal alignment and calm. You must be honest with yourself before you choose what is best for yourself.

Tossing a label, like midlife crisis, on an action that is sad or painful diminishes the opportunity for individuals to be responsible. It creates a closed conversation excuse that often leaves the individual open to repeat transgressions with themselves and others. It creates a cycle of pain, unwillingness to heal and grow, and lack of intentionality.

Again, take a deep breath. I have never had an affair. Still, it is a complicated topic. Even the complicated topics deserve consideration as the notion of midlife crisis is dismantled, or at the very least challenged. Are you beginning to think of moments when you questioned whether someone was having a midlife crisis? Are there unspoken areas of your life you have questioned and are now open to a new perspective? Keep being curious! Stretch beyond what you have known up until now. It is possible you have also experienced midlife calm or are on the cusp of stepping into this space!

Breaking a cycle can feel uncomfortable. Have you ever known someone who wanted to stop smoking? People try all kinds of strategies: the patch, gum, hypnosis, and more. They are committed to breaking their habit to realize a bigger, brighter reality for themselves. And it is often awkward and cumbersome.

There is a simple exercise I share with clients and offer you now. Open both your hands so your fingers are stretched open. Place your hands a foot apart, with your palms facing one another. Fold your hands together and allow your fingers to interlock. Now, unlock your fingers and pull your hands apart so there is a foot between your two palms again. Quickly repeat this action of clasping your hands together and reopening them. Repeat a dozen times.

On the last time, keep your hands clasped together and notice where your left thumb is located. Is it on top of or below your right thumb? I am willing to bet it was in the same placement the first eleven times you clasped your hands together.

Repeat this exercise. This time, place your left thumb differently… if it was on the bottom the past dozen times, place it on the top. If it was on the top, place it below your right thumb. Quickly clasp and pull apart your hands a dozen times with your thumbs in the new position.

This is a simple exercise of shifting from one way to a new way. It feels different. Not bad, just different. This is the way of transition. It is surprising and exciting to recognize how quickly we adapt to and embrace new ways.

This is also true for midlife calm. It may at first seem challenging, like quitting smoking. This is especially true when midlife calm feels forced upon you. Or it may feel awkward like the clasped hand exercise. In either case, aligning to your inner intention – your inner truth – is the compass that guides you through moments of discomfort. It truly is possible to create a new way forward.

When I was in my teens, I had to create a new way forward. Perhaps you did too. It happened around the age of sixteen when I got my first car. To be clear, it was the car my parents allowed me to use to get back and forth from school. This was helpful to them as my commitments often overlapped with their work schedules. It was also massively helpful to me to have this new freedom!

For sixteen years I did not drive, and then I did. I remember feeling stressed the first few times I drove over the bridge connecting east Toledo to downtown. Though every part of me wanted to curl up and retract, I quickly learned to flow with the four lanes of traffic.

That is how it goes when we transition from one way to another. We commit to a goal and move through the steps to arrive at it. Whether it is a simple exercise of clasping our hands together, learning to drive, or stepping into midlife calm, we have all the tools we need to land exactly where our heart, mind, and being is calling us.

I have one more exercise for you.

This is powerful in any moment of life, yet for those feeling the calm cast upon them this may be especially meaningful.

Stand with your feet together, pointed forward. Raise your dominant arm to shoulder height and extend your pointer finger so it is pointing directly in front of you. Without straining or shifting the position of your feet, move your pointer finger clockwise as far as your body will easily turn. Notice where your pointer finger ended in this experience. Did your arm rotate one-hundred degrees? One-hundred and sixty degrees? More? Less? Just notice where you ended.

Go ahead and put this book down to complete the first part of the exercise.

Great! Next, return to your initial position, with your arms hanging at the sides of your body. Close your eyes. This time, without raising or rotating your arm, simply visualize the same process. Feel your feet firmly anchored in place. Visualize your arm raising from the side of your body and pointing to a spot in front of you. Picture yourself slowly rotating your body, without moving your feet. Visualize yourself rotating with ease an additional twenty-five percent beyond where you landed the first time. Notice how easy it was to extend further. Smile at yourself.

Again, pause before reading further. Close your eyes and visualize the second part of this exercise.

Now for the final step. Start from your initial position, this time with your eyes open again. Repeat the action: raise your arm, point your finger out in front of you. This time, with the most recent visualization present, rotate your body as far as is comfortable without moving or shifting your feet. Notice where your finger is pointing.

What was your result? Did you go any further than the first time?

People typically rotate ten to twenty-five percent further after the visualization step. This teaches us that our unconscious limitations are real, and they often hold us back. Visualizing and creating a clear intention are powerful exercises. It enables us to stretch beyond our previous limitations. This is especially important when we are suffering a loss or other form of unsolicited midlife calm. We actually are capable of more – more joy, energy, possibility, calm.

If you are in a midlife calm that was not intentionally chosen, give yourself permission to heal and to be supported. If you are in a midlife calm that is a powerful and deliberate choice, give yourself permission to go all the way in creating the life that lights you up!

Whichever situation you may find yourself, take a moment to picture being in a state of calm. How does your body feel? What expression is on your face? How do you interact with others? Give yourself permission to practice and play with bringing your vision to life.

Life will not be perfect. There will be tangles and tensions. Yet, in the wise words of the poet Mary Oliver, this is our one wild and precious life.[56] We get to choose how we act and react, how we show up or stand down, what our intention is, and how we step into committed action. The chance to forge new cultural norms and shift from old stories to vision is upon us. It does not matter if you are in midlife or some other season of life. This is our opportunity. Life is happening for you, not to you. Life is now.

nine

The concept of momentum landed for me during a session with my personal trainer in 2020. I was laying on a bench to lift free weights for upper body resistance training. It required attention to form and movement. By the second set, with increased weight, I noticed and shared how hard it was to lift the weight. Nic, incredibly skilled at his trade, consistently challenged me but never pushed too hard. With his help and a slight adjustment to my positioning, I slowly lifted the weight. By the third rep, I was in a rhythmic flow of extending and retracting my bicep. Such a simple reality, but a lightbulb turned on in that moment. Momentum!

Newton's First Law of Motion states that a body in motion stays in motion.[57] A body at rest stays at rest until an outside force acts on it. These are scientific realities. And there I was, a grown adult who had not yet honored the wisdom of this truth. The wedge representing physical health and movement on my Wheel of Life would be scored as a five out of ten and halfway colored in. What occurred to me that day was that a body in slow movement is…a body in slow movement. It was better than being completely stopped, but it was not the life I craved.

For me, being in slow-motion physically represented never going to the mountaintops or the valleys. I was simply plodding through life – nothing too high or too low. I was robbing myself of radiant beauty. I realized if I did not step into intentional action, I was doomed to a life of mediocrity.

Intellectually, I was a body in motion. I had completed undergraduate and graduate degrees and continued to pursue certifications and trainings. Emotionally, I could cry, laugh, and express a full range of emotions. Again, a body in motion. Spiritually, I sporadically attended church, although did not have a practice of prayer that I exercised with any rhythm or consistency. So spiritually, I was in stop/start motion. This made the initial effort a heavy lift every time, just like the weights.

What could happen in your life if you built a momentum of calm? I believe midlife calm can become such a perpetual motion and flow that you short-circuit the momentum of crisis. Certainly, if given a choice of being disrupted by calm or by chaos, I choose calm every time! Are you with me?

I am prepared to go on record and say that our culture has reached a tipping point. We have evolved to a point where we get to live in a way that is deliberate and meaningful. We get to embrace crisis as an opportunity, not a debilitating deficit. With an intention of growth and a sense of curiosity, midlife gets to be a season we run toward rather than away from.

If Elliot Jaques created the concept of Midlife Crisis in 1965, then we can create the concept of Midlife Calm in 2022.

Imagine the story being told like this:

You are born. You grow up with all you need and much of what you want. You create connections and community, often through sports, music, church, and the neighborhood where you live. You arrive at school and learn in a way that celebrates your curious mind and active body. Experiential learning creates synergy. You give your best because it is fun. You graduate from twelve years of school. You proceed to trade school, college, or secure a job. You are now an adult.

You have structures in place to support your stretching, growing, and milestones ahead. You are interested in extending your own wings. You are encouraged by your family, friends, and colleagues to continue to develop into the leader and contributor that you are. You start making money and begin to feel the excitement of freedom that comes with financial reward. There is temptation to go overboard, indulge, and overspend. Perhaps you do. Then you are coached by those who love you to follow a path that offers valuable lessons, versus an aimless path that leads into a spiral of confusion, stress, tension, and debt.

You feel the tension between doing, having, and being. The practice of noticing has been engrained within you. You do not judge or compare yourself. Rather, you notice how the tension feels and make decisions based on the multitude of new opportunities pouring in. Some decisions seem to lead to peace, fulfillment, and calm. Others lead to stress, contradiction, and isolation. These are your choices. This is your life. You choose peace, fulfillment, and calm.

Then perhaps you attract a person who excites and startles you all at once. The startling factor is the blend of support and challenge this person brings to your life. You are all in. That other person is all in. Together, you create a life that reflects who you both are and reinforces your choice of calm. You align with work that fulfills you, offers the financial abundance you seek, and empowers you to invest ample time in this person with whom you are creating a life. Perhaps little humans are added to the mix. At any moment, you gaze around your space to see love, connection, playfulness, and authenticity. You are living your calm.

With each passing year, you continue to engage in choices that stimulate you physically, intellectually, emotionally, and spiritually. Along the way, you buy the car you have always wanted. You travel the countryside. You donate to your favorite charitable causes. You have family game nights and potluck dinners. You live the life you imagine!

When you find yourself struggling in your commitment to your partner, you notice and realign. When you go overboard in any area of life, you recalibrate. It is possible because you know yourself. You know what calm looks, feels, smells, tastes, and sounds like. Calm is your north star.

At some point, you choose to shift your attention from routine work to volunteerism or caring for others. These connections feed you. You are aging and see how deeply valuable you are to your family, community, and the world. Your wisdom has no limitations. You are living your calm in every moment. You contribute and thrive at every stage of life. Life has indeed offered you some unsolicited opportunities to practice the calm. You accepted the invitation and practiced through disease, career shifts, and death. You committed to rigor as well as ease.

These moments brought you into deeper acknowledgement of your power and gifts. You are amazed at how rich your life is. You were able to live every moment. You have breathed deeply. You trusted yourself, sought support, and remained open to receiving, growing, and stretching. And you are not even done.

The rhythm of life has you positioned to share the calm with your children's children. You talk to them about who they are and the gifts they bring to the world. You show them what it looks like to goof up and realign. You cherish them as humans who can also choose, live, and experience finding their own flavor of calm. By living it, you model it. By modeling it, you instill it in others. By instilling it in others, you create a lineage of calm. A culture of calm.

How does that version of the story land within you? Who do you get to be to cause and create this reality, or your own version?

I do not pretend to have all the answers. Rather, I am here to offer ideas to support your evolution. The following strategies build and elevate calm. These strategies are not all inclusive, rather are excellent starting points. Each requires commitment, consistency, and practice. What I find especially exciting is that you get to create and share your wisdom! This is how we grow into our calm as individuals, community, and society.

Notice without judgement or comparison
Noticing is the experience of turning inward. In noticing, you offer attention to the thoughts floating through your mind and how your body is responding. Noticing is not agreeing or disagreeing with the thoughts or feelings. It is simply an awareness. No judgement. No comparison. Acknowledge what is stirring within you. It will allow you to move through and forward.

Language speaks loudly
Humans are meaning-making machines. Your language evokes powerful responses, whether positive, negative, or neutral. Your words, inflection, and tone set you up for excellence, mediocrity, or failure. Choose your language wisely. Intentionally use words

that propel you and others forward instead of holding you back. Keep your eyes open and be person-centered.

Your stories are powerful

What stories are you telling yourself and others? What stories are you believing and embodying? Have you agreed to uphold cultural norms above your own well-being and happiness? Stories are powerful, and so are you. Pay attention to whether your stories create a life you love or a life you resist. Choose to believe and tell the stories that support and empower you.

Be a person of vision and intention

Intention allows you to be invested in the present and future, rather than fixated on the past. One does not drive with their eyes fixed on the rear-view mirror. You get to live with forward vision. Setting intentions invites you to view the bigger picture and allows the mechanics to fall into place.

Look for clues

There are ample clues that can guide you toward your inner calm if you pay attention. These clues point you in the direction of your desires, your genius, and what works well for who you are. Sometimes the clue comes in the form of resistance. When there is resistance to a thought or action, you get to be curious. You get to explore why you are resistant, and whether it is indeed your inner voice guiding you to comply or shift. Other times a clue comes in the form of ease and flow. Invite and embrace these moments as you deeply experience your calm.

Stretch beyond your comfort zone

When was the last time you stretched beyond your comfort zone? Did you panic and retreat when you were surrounded by fear, or did you lean into learning and growth? Stepping outside your comfort zone challenges your safety and control. However, often you will find there is nothing actually uncomfortable. Unfamiliar? Sure. Yet there are also great gifts to be found when you stretch beyond your comfort zone.

Operate from the whole

Operating from the whole requires stepping beyond the prescribed message of who you should be, what you should do, how you should think and feel, and how you should act. It is honoring the parts of you that have been dormant and inviting them to come out and play. It releases the limitations placed on you by others, society, and yourself. Operating from the whole is honoring that opposite forces, like yin and yang, may in fact be interdependent, interconnected, and complementary.

Trust your inner voice

Your inner voice can serve as a compass if you allow it. It is always ready to speak when you are ready to listen. This voice is pure and honest, free of the confusion and clutter created by external noise. Take some time in stillness, pose a question, and then be present. Your inner voice will speak from your best and highest self.

Valleys and mountaintops

Just as life is full of highs and lows, midlife calm can arrive in either space. Yet even when you find yourself in the shadows of the valleys of life you can experience beauty and gifts. You simply need to remain open to the possibility and use the tools available. Without going high or low, you may miss an opportunity to live a life that is uniquely yours.

Learn from others

There are as many approaches to living a life of fulfillment and contribution as there are cultures on the globe. It is not necessary to figure everything out yourself. There is beauty in learning from the genius of others. There is power in requesting and receiving support. Reframing language and cultivating diverse habits is a powerful strategy to accelerate your growth.

Your five senses

Focusing on each of your five senses grounds you in the present. What do you smell, feel, hear, see, and taste? What reaction does each create in you? What emotion or memory is brought forward? Practicing being connected to your senses can be done anytime, anywhere. Your senses are powerful grounding tools to bring you to the here and now.

Consistency and committed action

There is no destination. Your life is a journey full of twists, turns, and adventures. The goal is to consistently practice attuning and aligning within yourself. Life is a continual process of getting clear with your intentions and allowing the mechanics to flow from that space. Whenever you deviate from your path, you get to course correct in the moment. This is the work of consistency and committed action. This is the work of daily, and perhaps moment by moment, baby steps toward your intention and vision. These baby steps of consistent action grow into steady strides and ultimately miles traversed toward who you are created to be. Your consistent, committed action gets to be imperfect. The next best step is all that is required to live your midlife calm.

Dance!

Life – and midlife calm – gets to be fun! Whether you stoke your inner fire by dancing, laughing, telling jokes, creating art, or jogging…do it often! Create spaces for play, celebration, and joy. The simple act of physically moving your body will shift the brain into knowing you are on the move. In stretching beyond your current scenario, you become aligned with yourself and your calling.

My friend, your story is not fully written. It is up to you.

Imagine for a moment: what story would you like for your life? Set down your burdens and truly give this question some consideration. Go big. Be bold. Live audaciously! Allow the first idea that comes to mind to nestle into your heart and fill your entire being. Let it grow. Invite that notion to dance within you. Let the idea that starts as a spark grow into a fire of vision and intention. This spectacular story you are conjuring up is for you. It is your inner voice speaking wisdom of what to pursue.

You were created for greatness. If you already embrace this truth, keep going. If you are considering this idea for the first time, take a step toward this truth.

As you explore and practice the strategies shared in this chapter, my invitation is to look for the calm. You are more likely to find what you are looking for. Allow your curiosity about midlife calm to stretch into your conversations. Invite others to be intrigued. Celebrate your calm because when you celebrate, it increases. And when you arrive at midlife calm, healing occurs.

Midlife calm is available to you. Today, tomorrow, and every day forward. Come join me! It is time to create a midlife calm movement!

Epilogue and Call to Action

The intention I set for this book is to create curiosity in individuals, spark conversations, cultivate new paradigms, shift cultural norms, and heal our world.

This intention extends far beyond the pages of this book though. As a person enthralled with community and macro level change, I used to believe this looked like massive overhauls of programs and services. Through the years however, I have learned that curiosity, conversations, healing, new paradigms and shifted cultural norms happen one human at a time. So now that you have read *Midlife Calm*, I would like to invite you to join me in making this intention a reality.

I have a vision of midlife calm being a conversation that inspires people to recalibrate – to align within. My vision is for people to have permission to fully embrace who they are and celebrate those around them for who they are as well. My vision is for individuals to show up as powerful, intimate, authentic, vulnerable, compassionate, courageous, playful, and endless other ways of being. It is time for you and me – and the whole world – to embrace and celebrate that we are human beings… not human doings!

Let's start a Midlife Calm movement! That's right – my invitation to you is to be curious, start talking, heal, and shift. This will require you, me, hundreds of humans and whole communities to be open to possibilities. This call to action looks like tuning into your five senses, altering your language to support what you are up to, and stretching into your learning and growth zones.

It looks like requesting and receiving support and being vulnerable enough to learn from others.

This call to action looks like is prioritizing the questions, *"Who are you?"* and *"Who do you want to be?"* when we engage with ourselves and others. It requires each of us to practice answering those two questions and get familiar with who we are and what we are up to causing and creating in life.

As you enter or explore your midlife calm, my invitation is to share your story, and invite others to do the same. Through sharing, we get to learn from one another and create a new way that supports us.

My team and I have created a platform to gather and showcase stories of midlife calm. So, share your experience in whatever medium inspires. you. Perhaps your midlife calm is best expressed in the form of a piece of art, a culinary delight, a song, a sculpture, an athletic endeavor, a story. Whatever form it takes, your voice – your story – is vital to creating this movement.

Please visit:

PotereCoaching.com/midlife-calm

Check out the gallery of others' midlife calm moments and stories and please, take the opportunity to submit yours. I can hardly wait to hear from you!

Thank you for joining me in this vision and commitment to midlife calm.

Acknowledgements

My Family of Origin:

Mom and Dad, you are role models of calm. When life is high, low, or hectic, you ground yourselves and move forward. By showing up as your loving, generous, compassionate, creative, connected selves, you have taught me that calm is not only possible, it is necessary and transformative. I finally get it because you are consistent, courageous, and authentic.

Patrice, I see the way you create space for relationships and self-care. I see you showing up with love and creativity. I see you, sister. It is the honor of a lifetime to be on this journey of living, loving, and growing with you.

My Family of Choice:

Elaine Higgins, Xavier University friends and faculty, Jesuit Volunteer Corps, my communities at the University of Michigan and in Covington, Kentucky, and countless humans who have blessed me throughout life:

Each of you have seen me through mountaintop moments of joy and valley periods of sorrow. You draw me into my gifts and call forth my greatness. Thank you for loving me in such powerfully present ways. You are the reason I commit to living my calm.

Candace Klein Sjogren: This book would not be here today if not for you and the Boston Breakthrough Academy. You stir my soul and evoke my vision, my superpowers, and my self-trust. Your journey inspires me beyond words. And as for the journey we are on together…watch out world!

Patrick Flerlage: I am filled with wonder and awe at how our paths have crossed and now fully united. Although I was well into my midlife calm, you enhance the adventure. You are a grounded presence, a safe space, and the dance partner I have always wanted. Life really is easy and fun with you!

My Editors:

Alec Quig, you have laser focus and a brilliant mind. Thank you for your honesty and rigor through this process. I suspect there is more to come!

Jess Cybrowski, Patrick Flerlage, Richard Hernandez, Myke Lewis, Danny Perkins, Dianne Powers, Thom Powers, Shannon Silk, Sara Smith. I trusted each of you with the early, rough manuscript of **Midlife Calm**. The encouragement you offered propelled my vision and gave me permission to be messy in the process. Thank you for your unwavering candor and support. Having you on my team makes me courageous and confident.

My Friends who Contributed:

Ehab Abdalla, Marianne Bailey, Monica Dennison, Richard Danford, Yohanna Estime, Gonzalo Hernandez, Lynda Jackson, MaryBeth Lacy, Zia Maumenee, Jean Meyer, Candice Nonas, Jenn Payeur, Donyatta Price Strong, Sunshine Richards, Susan Robinson, Brett Sears, Richard

Shepard, Paul Syzmanski, Lisa Tipis, Ron Tremblay, Carole Varanelli, Hunter Warne, and Bob Young. Your perspectives about midlife crisis informed my process and escalated my commitment to this book. Thank you for being committed to me and my vision.

My Publishing Team:

Claire Long: You came into my life like a burst of light and love at the most miraculous time. Our conversations over a lobby countertop invigorated me and ultimately pointed me to the most magical publishing experience I could imagine. Thank you for being such a generous and supportive soul.

Brian Shircliff and VITALITY buzz, bliss + books: Your intention of transforming lives through gentle and accessible self-care is beautifully evident. You are permission to show up exactly as I am. You remind me that everything is possible! It is an honor to be invited into and embraced by you and this community of beautiful humans.

Notes

Chapter One

1 (2021, June 8). Best Zoo. USA Today 10 Best. https://www.10best.com/awards/travel/zoo/

2 Syme, R. (2017, November 25). *Hooray for Fiona the Hippo, Our Bundle of Social-Media Joy.* New York Times. https://www.nytimes.com/2017/11/25/style/fiona-the-hippo.html

3 Curley, M. (2016, April 22). *Cincinnati Zoo Nationally Recognized for Sustainability Efforts.* Cincinnati Zoo & Botanical Garden. https://cincinnatizoo.org/news-tag/greenest-zoo-in-america/

4 WLWT Digital Staff (2019, March 15). *Cincinnati Scientists help birth first -ever jaguar created by artificial insemination.* https://www.wlwt.com/article/cincinnati-scientists-help-birth-first-ever-jaguar-created-by-artificial-insemination/26824724#:~:text=CINCINNATI%20%E2%80%94%20Scientists%20from%20the%20Cincinnati%20Zoo%20are,scientific%20advancement%20for%20the%20conservation%20of%20this%20species.

5 Curley, M. (2021, July 29). *Cincinnati Zoo and Community Partners put final touches on Rockdale Academy Urban Learning Garden.* Cincinnati Zoo & Botanical Garden. https://cincinnatizoo.org/news-releases/cincinnati-zoo-and-community-partners-put-final-touches-on-rockdale-academy-urban-learning-garden/

6 Brownfield, A. (2021, June 20). *Cincinnati Zoo's $150M Expansion designed to make it a '10 our of 10'.* Cincinnati Business Courier. https://www.bizjournals.com/cincinnati/news/2021/06/20/zoos-150m-expansion-designed-to-make-it-a.html

7 Curley, M. Cincinnati Zoo, Plan your Visits, Manatee Springs. https://cincinnatizoo.org/plan-your-visit/exhibits/manatee-springs/

Chapter Two

[8] Midlife Crisis. (2022). In Wikipedia. https://en.wikipedia.org/wiki/Midlife_crisis

[9] Jaques, E. (1965). Death and the mid-life crisis. *The International Journal of Pyscho-Analysis,* Volume 46, 502.

[10] Haslam, N. (2019, January 6). *Is the 'midlife crisis' a real thing?* The Conversation. https://theconversation.com/is-the-midlife-crisis-a-real-thing-105510#:~:text=The%20psychoanalyst%20Elliot%20Jaques%2C%20who,%2C%20becomes%20a%20personal%20matter%E2%80%9D.

[11] Jaques, E. (2006) *Death and the mid-life crisis* (1st ed.).

[12] (2021) *The notion of the midlife crisis,* Chamberlain College of Nursing, Psychology 4146. https://www.coursehero.com/file/67240467/midlife-crisispdf/

[13] Carl Jung. (2022). In Wikipedia. https://en.wikipedia.org/wiki/Carl_Jung

[14] *Erikson's 8 Stages of Psychosocial Development,* Lumen Learning, Part II: Educational Psychology. https://courses.lumenlearning.com/teachereducationx92x1/chapter/eriksons-stages-of-psychosocial-development/

[15] Daniel Levinson (2020). In Wikipedia. https://en.wikipedia.org/wiki/Daniel_Levinson#:~:text=Research%20%26%20Theory,-Stage%2Dcrisis%20view&text=Levinson%20believed%20that%20the%20pre,made%20up%20a%20person's%20life.

[16] Stage-crisis view (2022). In Wikipedia. https://en.wikipedia.org/wiki/Stage-crisis_view

[17] Freund, A.M. & Ritter, J.O. (2009). Midlife Crisis: A Debate. *Gerontology, Behavioural Science Section,* 55, 582-591.

[18] Italie, H. (2020, August 25). *Writer Gail Sheehy, author of landmark best-seller 'Passages' , dies at 83,* USA Today. https://www.usatoday.com/story/entertainment/books/2020/08/25/writer-gail-sheehy-author-passages-dies-83/3438599001/

[19] O'Toole, J. et. al. (1972, December). Work in America. Report of a Special Task Force to the Secretary of health, education, and welfare. Department of Health, Education, and Welfare. 1 – 228. https://files.eric.ed.gov/fulltext/ED070738.pdf

[20] Sheehy, Gail (1996). *New Passages: Mapping Your Life Across Time.* Collins. ISBN 978-0-00-255619-4.

[21] Freund, A.M. & Ritter, J.O. (2009). Midlife Crisis: A Debate. *Gerontology, Behavioural Science Section*, 55, 582-591.

[22] Schaie, K. W. & Willis, S. L. (1986). *Adult development and aging.* (National Library of Medicine). (2nd Ed.). Boston: Little, Brown.

[23] Freund, A.M. & Ritter, J.O. (2009). Midlife Crisis: A Debate. *Gerontology, Behavioural Science Section*, 55, 582-591.

[24] Hunter, S., & Sundel, M. (Eds.). (1989). *Midlife myths: Issues, findings, and practice implications.* Sage Publications, Inc.

[25] U.S. Department of Health and Human Services. *Midlife in the United States.* National Institute on Aging. https://www.nia.nih.gov/research/resource/midlife-united-states

[26] Helson, R. and Wink, P. (1992, April). Personality Change in Women from the early 40s to the early 50s. *Psychology and Aging.* 7(1). 46 – 55.

[27] Costa, P.T., Herbst, J.H., McCrae, R.R., and Siegler, I.C. (2000, December 1). Personality at Midlife: Stability, Intrinsic Maturation, and Response to Life Events. *Sage Journals, PubMed.* https://journals.sagepub.com/doi/abs/10.1177/107319110000700405

[28] Aldwin, C.M, Levenson, M.R. *Stress, Coping, and Health at Mid-life: A Developmental Perspective.* From The Handbook of Midlife Development. New York: Wiley. 1 – 29.

[29] Lachman, M.E. (2004). Development in midlife. *Annual Review Psychology.* PubMed. (55). 305-331.

[30] Brim, O.G. Jr. (1976). Theories of the male mid-life crisis. *Counseling Psychologist.* 6(1). 2 – 8.

[31] Martin, M., Rocke, C., Willis, S.L. (2010, September 14). Longitudinal perspectives on midlife development: stability and change. *European Journal of Aging* 7. 131 – 134.

Chapter Four

[32] (2022). Belief. *MacMillian Dictionary*. https://www.macmillandictionary.com/us/thesaurus-category/american/to-believe-or-accept-that-something-is-true-or-exists

[33] (2022). Thought. *MacMillian Dictionary*. https://www.macmillandictionary.com/us/dictionary/american/thought_1 M.R.

[34] (2021, September 2). *Dementia*. World Health Organization. https://www.who.int/news-room/fact-sheets/detail/dementia

[35] Dilallo, F.A., Powers, T., Bartholomew, L. (2018, March 12). *Peace be with you: A Christian Solution to Bullying. Grades 4-8 Curriculum*. Consulting & Training Services LLC. 24 – 28.

[36] Christel, D.A. and Dunn, S.C. (2016, August 5). Average American woman's clothing size: comparing national health and nutritional examination surveys (1988-2010) to ASTM International Misses & women's plus size clothing. *International Journal of Fashion Design*. 10 (2). 129 – 136.

[37] Hendry, E.R. (2013, November 20). *7 Epic fails brought to you by the genius mind of Thomas Edison*. Smithsonian Magazine. https://www.smithsonianmag.com/innovation/7-epic-fails-brought-to-you-by-the-genius-mind-of-thomas-edison-180947786/

[38] Holmgren, M. (2021, April 26). *The truth about midlife crisis*. The Well by Northwell. https://thewell.northwell.edu/aging/midlife-crisis

Chapter Five

[39] Zetlin, M. (2019, October 23). *Dancing benefits brain function teamwork and health, according to a neuroscience Ph.D.* Inc. https://www.inc.com/minda-zetlin/dancing-dance-benefits-brain-function-teamwork-health-peter-lovatt-phd.html

[40] Benzaken, H. (2018, October 1). *Dance like nobody's watching, science says it's good for you*. Goodnet. https://www.goodnet.org/articles/dance-like-nobodys-watching-science-says-its-good-for-you

Chapter Six

[41] Pillay, S. MD. (2018, March 14). *Can you rewire brain to get out of a rut? (Yes you can…).* Harvard Health Publishing. Harvard Medical School. Harvard Health Blog. https://www.health.harvard.edu/blog/rewire-brain-get-out-of-rut-2018030913253

[42] Ashworth, L. *What is the frequency of gratitude?* The Celebration Effect. https://thecelebrationeffect.com/what-is-the-frequency-of-gratitude/

[43] (2022). *Cognitive Behavior Therapy: What is CBT?* Psychology Tools. https://www.psychologytools.com/self-help/what-is-cbt/

[44] Robbins, T. [Motivation Video]. (2021, June). *Tony Robbins Motivation – Your Six Human Needs.* YouTube. https://video.search.yahoo.com/search/video;_ylt=AwrEze3uABBi4HQAVwNXNyoA;_ylu=Y29sbwNiZjEEcG9zAzE EdnRpZANBMDYzNF8xBHNlYwNwaXZz?p=tony+robbins+six+needs+of +individuals&fr2=piv-web&type=E211US1451G91370&fr=mcafee#id=4&vid-=0174333738223250304604 1f88ee8e84&action=view

[45] Yin and Yang. (2022). In Wikipedia. https://en.wikipedia.org/wiki/Yin_and_yang

[46] Legacy Staff. (2014, February 28). *The Rest of Paul Harvey's Story.* Legacy.com. https://www.legacy.com/news/the-rest-of-paul-harveys-story/

[47] (2019). Boston Breakthrough Academy. https://bostonbreakthroughacademy.com/

[48] Dayman, L. (2020, January 15). *Ikigai: The Japanese concept of finding purpose in life.* Savvy Tokyo. Health & Beauty, Lifestyle.

[49] Kavedzija, Dr. I. *The Japanese concept of Ikigai: Why purpose might be a better goal than happiness.* Blue Zones. https://www.bluezones.com/2021/04/the-japanese-concept-of-ikigai-why-purpose-might-be-a-better-goal-than-happiness/

[50] Godrey, M., Young, J., Shannon, R., et al. (2018, June). The Person, interactions and environment programme to improve care of people with dementia in hospital: a multisite study. *NIHR Journals Library, Southampton UK. Health Services and Delivery Research. 6* (23). Chapter 4.

[51] Yohn, D.L. (2018, October 2). *6 Ways to build a customer-centric culture.*

Harvard Business Review. https://hbr.org/2018/10/6-ways-to-build-a-customer-centric-culture

[52] Schneier, B. (2007, March 22). *Why the human brain is a poor judge of risk.* Wired. https://www.wired.com/2007/03/security-matters0322/

[53] (2019, December 27). *21/90 Rule in Progress.* Booksy Press.

[54] Sutton Ph.D., J. (2021, July 2). *How to apply the wheel of life in coaching.* Positive Psychology. https://positivepsychology.com/wheel-of-life-coaching/

Chapter Eight

[55] The only evidence-based grief recovery program in the world. (2021). https://www.griefrecoverymethod.com/

[56] Oliver, M. (2015). Poem 133: The Summer Day. *Dogs Songs: Poems.* Penguin Books.

Chapter Nine

[57] (2022, April 19). *Newton's Laws of Motion.* NASA. Glenn Research Center. https://www1.grc.nasa.gov/beginners-guide-to-aeronautics/newtons-laws-of-motion/

About the Author

Krista Powers offers over two decades of experience moving beyond surface solutions and diving into the deep work of innovation and transformation in healthcare, nonprofit, education, and business. As the CEO and Founder of Potere Coaching, Krista is dedicated to supporting individuals and organizations with tools to accomplish immediate momentum and enduring success.

Krista's career has offered opportunities in direct service, program development and evaluation, fundraising, and leadership with local, regional, and national audiences. She has been honored to keynote at conferences and seminars. She is a member of coaching teams for the Cincinnati Regional Chamber and Boston Breakthrough Academy. Additionally, Krista is invested in a spirit of community and engagement. She has served in elected office on her local school board, was humbled to be named a 40 Under 40 Honoree and was invited to create and teach a course at Xavier University. She delights in serving on the board for the Giving Voice Foundation. Through all these experiences, Krista has honed an ability to quickly assess pain points and growth opportunities for individuals and businesses and has routinely found herself positioned in organizational change management and coaching roles.

A proud graduate of Xavier University and the University of Michigan, Krista's degrees in social work paired with certification in the Grief Recovery Method and Coaching lend a unique lens to her strategy of coaching the power within individuals. Her approach to coaching C-Suite, mid-level, and emerging leaders in the workplace has resulted in improved human and financial capital. It has also resulted in amplified personal confidence and

COACHING YOUR POWER WITHIN

clarity. Krista is committed to the radical results that occur when leaders invest in 'being' as much as 'doing.'

Krista has been a primary caregiver for a partner as well as an integral part of care teams for many individuals. She has experienced being consumed and lost while caregiving and has learned how to grow in a way that has rekindled her mind, heart, and spirit.

With gratitude for her path and an understanding of her talents and life journey, Krista is energized to align her gifts and passion to empower individuals especially during important and transformational moments of life.

Personally, Krista shares her life with an amazing man and his daughters in Covington, Kentucky.

PotereCoaching.com

VITALITY is a circle of friends welcoming all, awakening each other, and reminding each other that we are Whole. Our affordable self-care programs invite everyone to move, to breathe, to rest, to contemplate, to grow...wherever each person begins their self-care journey, wherever and however they want to become.

vitalitycincinnati.org

VITALITY buzz, bliss + books LLC publishes books & creations from VITALITY's circle of friends to inspire love, creativity, + possibility:

A New Setting of the Spiritual Exercises: Hearing, Seeing, Feeling Old Stories in New Ways by the Companions of VITALITY

Selected Homilies: allowing life experience to open up the ways and the Word of God by Richard Bollman, S.J.

yoga is THE ALL: an invitation to sensational life by the Companions of VITALITY

With You in Our Dreams, a reading and coloring book for all ages by Mike Eck (poet) & Claire Long (artist)

Milford: A poet's life in spiritual retreat by Evan R. Underbrink

The Naked Path of Prophet series, including volume 0 *A Wildly Sensual YAHWEH* by Brian J. Shircliff

vitalitybuzz.org